The Classical Drama
of France

WILL G. MOORE

The Classical Drama of France

OXFORD UNIVERSITY PRESS
London   Oxford   New York
1971

Oxford University Press

OXFORD   LONDON   NEW YORK

GLASGOW   TORONTO   MELBOURNE   WELLINGTON

CAPE TOWN   SALISBURY   IBADAN   NAIROBI

DAR ES SALAAM   LUSAKA   ADDIS ABABA

BOMBAY   CALCUTTA   MADRAS   KARACHI   LAHORE   DACCA

KUALA LUMPUR   SINGAPORE   HONG KONG   TOKYO

PRINTED IN GREAT BRITAIN
BY BUTLER & TANNER LTD
FROME AND LONDON

FOR BARBARA
who read every chapter

Preface

READERS should be warned that the following pages attempt two things. They aim to present the actual state of knowledge concerning a well-known area of modern art. And they aim no less to suggest that research has not yet supplied us with any satisfactory key to this art form, that although we know much about it, we do not yet know the most important things about it. We do not know with any certainty how it began, what kept it alive, what caused its decline, what it has contributed to art and to life.

I hope that my personal doubts about these matters, doubts which I do not ask my readers to share, may not confuse my account of the things which may be fairly be said to be known and agreed. But if I am right, the textbooks that our grandchildren will read may be as different from those we use now, as is our present knowledge when compared with that of a hundred years ago. I have tried to express this view in other works, and I regret that it has seemed to give offence to some scholars. I would welcome an opportunity of assuring them (and any others who detect an element of arrogance in my repeated suggestion that we do not understand the past) that I hope at least that such an element is not decisive. If I have suggested a 'new criticism' of Molière in one of my books, and in articles have explored 'new readings' of French classics, that is not because I claim insights withheld from my professional colleagues. No pupil of Lucien Febvre and of Gustave Rudler could fail to develop a natural scepticism as to his knowledge of the past. We know very little of what, and of how, things happened: the so-called 'facts' that are handed down to later generations are, both in extent and in importance, a tiny part of the abundant life that once was. As long as we make things worse by studying the past in watertight compartments, we cannot hope to recover anything like the real state of things. The young seem to demand this more insistently than their elders. Their desire for broader study programmes reflects, I think, a quite sound instinct, which is to study the art of the past in a rich context of social history and the development of ideas. We have books about books, as Montaigne remarked: they tell us about editions, texts; they claim to trace influences; but they do not tell us how formative minds read the books at their disposal. Can we claim to understand French classical literature as long as we do not know *how* Voltaire read Pascal? So often we seem even unaware of the question: *what* Voltaire read is surely of less import in a final count than what he looked for, what he missed, what made him think.

The debate about the nature of classicism, in which this little book is involved, has probably not yet reached the decisive stage. What is here written is no more than one man's testimony. Thirty years of teaching have only enforced my conviction that we should take as essential starting-point the surely not very extraordinary premiss that the works of the chief French classical writers have kept their vitality because they are the product of powerful imagination. If we will only grant so much, then things like rules and dramatic conventions fall into their subordinate place. This means (I know) that such a work as René Bray's *Formation de la doctrine classique* ceases to be an essential textbook, since its information is correct but its priorities are wrong.

Even more difficulties of approach are removed if we remind ourselves that classical drama is a highly artificial creation, involving rhetoric from the start. So that to call a play rhetorical, which in English is a derogatory epithet, is to describe it and not to condemn it. It is not in the least to say that a classical play may not involve deep and controversial issues. French plays do in fact raise some of the basic problems of modern living. All drama starts with convention; it may end with insights the more profound in that they are the result of art, and not of discussion or doctrine. As Louis Jouvet once wrote,

On commence par le brillant, le faux, le simulacre pour aller à une vie intérieure.

Such are some of the thoughts inspired by long study of problems of French civilization. But as I reflect upon such a study I am reminded of all that even so summary an account as this owes to the labours of others. Any real list of contributors to this book would begin with my first teachers, my parents; it would give prominent place to the stimulus and forbearance of my wife and children and grandchildren. It would include my students of all kinds and in two hemispheres. School audiences, for example, have helped me more than they could know, so have undergraduates, graduates, and colleagues. The actual text of this volume owes much to the encouragement and the criticism of Gaston Hall, W. D. Howarth, Christine Crow, P. J. Yarrow, and many another. It owes its material form to the patient and skilful typing of Miss Wade. I hope I may thank them here in a real sense. It is usual to say in a preface that for the faults of the book the author is alone responsible, and to that I conventionally conform.

W.G.M.

Contents

1
The Point of View

MOST people who care for drama recognize the sort of play we call classical, a play which relies for its effect on regularity of form, on unity of impression, and on absence of physical action. In it we expect to enjoy words and not to watch fisticuffs. Conflicts there are, as in all drama, but mental rather than physical, symbolic rather than realist. We watch a clash of opinions, of attitudes rather than of individuals; we hear a language which is rare rather than racy; we are not reminded of real life but allowed to escape from it.

For some people this is just not dramatic. Like Victor Hugo, in the heat of his romantic polemic against a classical form which had become rigid and frigid, they demand, not the 'elbows' of action but its 'hands', doing what hands can do, gripping, joining, strangling. They want localized action, in Sean O'Casey's Dublin, recognizable types as in *La Dame aux camélias*, the whiff of local politics as in Ibsen. Classical drama discards battles, disguises the act of murder; it prefers motives, mental struggle, spiritual depression or exaltation. It is usually poetic drama. Some of its features are seen in *Murder in the Cathedral*, almost all of them in *Samson Agonistes*.

Since even the word 'classical' is used ambiguously, it may be well to state now that in this book the word 'neo-classical' will not be used; the word 'classic' will be kept to describe an outstanding or well-known example: we speak for instance of a 'classic' case, or of a film as a classic, of *Faust* as a classic. The word 'classical' has in modern usage two meanings: the first refers to regularity of style, as in a building or in a poem, and the second to a style that derives from what European education knows as the classical cultures of Greece and Rome. This confusion, or more strictly fusion, of meaning hides much cultural history. A classical building is regular and well proportioned; it is also in fact in the Greek or the Roman style. Thus Euripides is thought of as classical in both senses. This common respect for the authors of Greece and Rome, who are thought of as 'classics', that is as works which set tone and pattern, is so deeply embedded in the European tradition that it describes qualities which those authors are thought to have had in peculiar measure. This suggests questions of tradition and influence in European art which our present instruments seem unable to make fully clear. A Japanese observer might pertinently ask how far such qualities as the sense of form and symmetry, awareness of proportion, universality, harmony have appealed to the European mind because they were connected with the authority of Greek and Roman prototypes in Western education.

This book studies a single case of such appeal, a form of drama which shows these 'classical' features but which does not demonstrably arise by imitation of Greek or Roman models. Yet whenever men attempted any critical assessment of this drama, the yardstick and standard by which it was measured was Aristotle or Seneca. Was this due to the fact that Europeans knew no other standard, or to acceptance of the inspired authority of Aristotle in all branches of thought?

It is a pity that a modern student, if he sets about study of drama, has to read a book. A play inevitably becomes a thing to be read. We learn to absorb it as we do a novel: we follow a sequence of words. We try to understand what the 'writer' has put down, in print, and we examine the print, in order to gauge its cogency, its inconsequence, its features, its images, its style. Surely this is unfair, to the play no less than to the playwright. Perhaps we have forgotten how contrary to the nature of drama it is to read, in a book, by oneself, something that was created to be heard and seen by people in company. No one can study drama who cannot read. But the illiterate, and the semi-literate, can enjoy acting. Molière was trained in a school where the actor both animated a situation and recited a script. The play's the thing, but in Hamlet's day the play was live action more than it is now. The public would not fault the actor, as now, for murdering his text, but for failing to convey the illusion and the pleasure of passion, and of suspense. The French classical drama that we are setting out to study is not book drama only. It was created to please many sorts and conditions of men:

A seventeenth-century audience likes theatre for its life and enthusiasm, its exaggerations and all that does not go along with the rules. If given its head this public would admit even the bloody and the obscene. We seem at times to forget that it is for such a public that drama is made. Dramatic writing is the only kind of writing in the seventeenth century that interests every kind of audience, because it is not confined to one class: to go to the theatre you need not be able to read.

(J. SCHERER, *Dramaturgie classique* (n.d. [1950]), p. 433)

So much modern drama is the reverse of classical in the profusion of its effects—spectacle, music, acrobatics, crowds, costumes—that we tend to think of classical drama in terms of what it does not offer, as bare and denuded of effects which we find elsewhere. This again is distortion. Every feature of classical drama is designed to offer a new kind of pleasure, a pleasure greater than realistic forms can offer. Its stylized language is more suggestive, not less, than everyday speech. Its rhetoric and its verse suggest more, and not less, than prosaic language can do. Its stress on credibility (*vraisemblance*) and on taste (*bienséance*) are meant to remove features which might shock and hinder us from entering fully into a most carefully designed illusion. The unities are means of concentration, of increasing our pleasure in the essence of an encounter or a mental state, by removing contingent and disturbing factors of time and place and irrelevance. I think that Voltaire had this in mind when he compared the suggestion of a silent night in Shakespeare and Racine. The sentry's words in *Hamlet* 'Not a mouse stirring' seemed to him soldier's language. In the famous line from *Iphigénie* he could hear the voice of a poet: 'Mais tout dort, et l'armée, et les vents, et Neptune.'

It would seem to be a question of taste: one likes this and another likes that. But this is not so. We are not reduced to a single form of dramatic pleasure, nor were mid-seventeenth-century Parisians. They could get one kind of thrill from the comedians of the Pont

Neuf, another from the tragic bombast of the Hotel de Bourgogne, yet another from the Italians, and still another from Molière, who shared their theatre.* When he tired of mime or slapstick the Parisian could take rhetoric, and with it the conventions of rhythmical speech. It would not disturb his pleasure to reflect that in real life we do not speak in verse, or speak to ourselves. A monologue would show him the inside of a mind, the clash of motive, the immortal longings of a fabulous queen, the sort of pleasure, perhaps, that Shakespeare's lines had given in London sixty years earlier:

> Between the acting of a dreadful thing
> And the first motion, all the interim is
> Like a phantasma, or a hideous dream:
> The genius and the mortal instruments
> Are then in council; and the state of man,
> Like to a little kingdom, suffers then
> The nature of an insurrection.
> (*Julius Caesar*, II. i. 63 ff.)

This is not to say, of course, that *Julius Caesar* is a classical play. What it does tell us is that the English audience liked a mixture of styles. It liked the illusion of daily ordinariness into which the poetry of meaning might break unawares, and depart as suddenly. The French audience liked one thing at a time, in this case words, grand words, suggesting, not what they knew too well already, but another world, a world of great persons beset by great conflicts. They liked grand attitudes, and they liked them the more when linked to grand speech: 'Ma plus douce espérance est de perdre l'espoir.' . . . This is wit, such as the seventeenth century loved, but it is more than wit, since the euphony of its words matches the intensity of a suggested situation. Corneille supplied such thrills in

* This fact seems to me more important than my text suggests. Molière's association with Italian players may be thought symbolic, for it put him in touch with ancient sources of European comedy. The point is put with both force and discretion by Thelma Niklaus in her *Harlequin Phoenix* (1956). See in particular her analysis of the commedia dell'arte (pp. 37 ff.: 'the only form of masked theatre known to modern Europe') and of its primary characters, Pantalone, Arlecchino, Brighella . . . Il Dottore, Pulcinello, Il Capitano, Scaramuccia, Pagliaccio, etc. All these were known to Molière and his public and must be reckoned a powerful ingredient of French classical comedy.

nearly every play he wrote: 'Dans un si grand revers, que vous reste-t-il? Moi, dis-je, et c'est assez.'

We may assume that it was enough. Voltaire was not a naïve man, not likely to be satisfied with feeble drama. He found many faults in Corneille, but his testimony is the more reliable for that: 'On ne connaissait point encore, avant *Le Cid* de Corneille, ce combat des passions qui déchire le cœur, et devant lequel toutes les beautés de l'art ne sont que des beautés inanimées.' Voltaire is not alone in suggesting the power of this form of drama. Modern actors and audiences have shown that it is not yet exhausted, and that the emotional forces unleashed by dramatic speech have a long life. This is not drama for every taste; it is not drama that the student must like. On the other hand, it is not, as a Californian daily paper said of *Britannicus*, a musty museum piece, for students only.

'The weakness of modern drama is the lack of a convention.' Whether T. S. Eliot is right or not, his remark pinpoints the paradox that convention, which at first sight seems hindrance to the dramatist, is on the contrary the very opposite, a source of power. It allows the suggestion of what could not be expressed at all in plain terms. The master-convention of classical drama is not the verse form, nor the lack of physical action, nor the few characters: it is the use of rhetoric as dramatic medium. Until we have come to terms with rhetoric we cannot taste the delights and the potency of classical drama. The word has a bad reputation, carrying suggestion of artifice, of something which (since the Romantic era) has seemed opposed to the natural. In its first meaning, however, rhetoric is the art of good speaking and good writing; it aims rather at filling out nature than taking its place. The abuse of rhetoric, which is belief in words for their own sake, implying a confusion of saying something with doing something, has really little to do with style. In a mordant phrase André Gide castigates the French as being a people 'perdu par la rhétorique, habile à se payer de mots', but in French art rhetoric comes into its own. A French classical play is a marvel of language, used with most varying and varied subtlety; all effects are conveyed by speech. No other aid to expression, be it gesture, music, peripety, can replace language, as vehicle of both intelligence and emotion. The point has been well put with regard to the greatest of French classical artists, Jean Racine:

Racine's theatre is clearly not realistic. His alexandrines are not to be spoken as if they were prose and the language used by his characters is not that of normal conversation. His passionate drama is all the time expressed in a language more formal even than that used in Louis XIV's court. We can enjoy the elegance of this language as we might enjoy the splendid sets and costumes of tragedy. Indeed it would be difficult to enjoy seventeenth-century tragedy . . . if one could not stand elegant or pompous language.

(P. FRANCE, *Racine's Rhetoric* (1965), p. 242)

The reward of studying rhetoric is to watch the meeting-point of art and nature. It allows us to study a poet's use of art as a means of expressing nature. 'We can never know the respective importance of Art and Nature, artifice and spontaneity in Racine's writing' (ibid., p. 4). But this does not prevent our enjoyment of what rhetoric allows a poet to say. Rhetoric can transfix the temporal:

Honteux attachements de la chair et du monde
Que ne me quittez-vous, quand je vous ai quittés!

This, again, is what its age would call wit, but it is wit that carries poetic suggestion of a dramatic moment. It is uttered by an actor, but is not confined to any individual. We may all imagine, or even share, its poignant sense of the cost to be paid if one counts the world well lost. Classical drama offers us an almost endless series of comparable moments, memorable because they are imagined as uttered by great figures of the past, Alexander, Attila, Mary Queen of Scots, the Earl of Essex, Mithridates, by generals, queens, martyrs, all of them figures who can be imagined in crucial or desperate situations, faced with decisions which can most fittingly be conveyed in rhythmical language.

Study of this kind of drama must be ambivalent. For us who study, the text is our evidence: 'Language is always basic' (ibid., p. 4). Yet our study of the text will depend on our appreciation of the dramatic illusion, on our ability, if you will, to imagine ourselves before a stage. This illusion, as we have already said, is something much more complex than a text drawn up by a poet. Of all forms of literary art, drama calls for special methods of study, since it constantly escapes literature. It is a social art, depending for success on co-operation between the public (many people together in one place) and actors engaged in constructing an illusion. But the actors can only do this on the lines (and, in fact, in the actual words) given them by the author. Later generations have only the texts written by these authors, so drama is perforce (but perversely) studied as literature. The play, designed as a co-operative perform- ance, has become a book. In the case of the drama studied here the process has led to a real deformation of what happened. Books have been written about the playwrights, but only about those who became famous, the rest being (with some justification) regarded as unreadable (reading the play being the unavowed criterion). For most modern readers French classical drama has become synony- mous with the printed plays of Corneille, Molière, and Racine, 'explained' where possible by a theory or code of writing to which they were supposed to conform. It needed the herculean efforts of an American scholar to make us realize that the famous few depended on traditions established by the many, that the master- pieces are surrounded and overwhelmed (in mass) by a vast dramatic industry, and in fact that 'the classical age is thoroughly classical only for those who refuse to consider more than a portion of the facts'. It has needed research into actors and theatres to show us that what we had considered to be independent efforts of a poet were responses to conditions of performance and of declamation. Classical works that we had assumed to be typical of their age begin to look much more like protests and exceptions when replaced in their actual context of plays, romantic, fantastic, didactic, polemical. It has now emerged that the decisive role in the development of classical drama was probably that of the public, already described as turbulent, who paid for their pleasure and who presumably paid best for what they liked to watch. But, as we shall see, the actors too did more than recite a given text. There is evidence that they asked authors to supply the sort of speech that they were confident would go down well with their public. Even Racine was accused of writing plays for an actress.

It has taken years of research to remind us that there is an economic side to drama, and that it may have been decisive where we are accustomed to consider only personal decisions. The story of the Paris theatres during the seventeenth century is one of a struggle for bare existence, leading gradually to affluence. We read of an actress complaining in the thirties that the 'new' authors like the Corneille brothers were demanding so much in payment for plays that the actors had to take less. The five-year prohibition of *Tartuffe* faced Molière's company with the prospect of destitution, and forced him to write plays centred on a single role (his own), in order to stave off penury. Yet the actor won in the end, and seems to have become richer than the author. La Bruyère, writing in the late eighties, put the point in his graphic and bitter way: 'Le comédien, couché dans son carrosse, jette de la boue au visage de Corneille, qui est à pied.'

The creations of art are malleable material. They are at the mercy of the beholder. What pleases contemporaries may pass out of fashion. What is at first hardly understood may emerge as a masterpiece. Much depends on the point of view. French drama is a national product, critically underestimated by foreigners, officially admired so loud and long that to us the French seem to protest too much the perfections of their own plays. Before we trace the history of a form which has been so much admired, and so often decried, let us pause to ask what in the opinion of scholars this form of art has achieved. This achievement has never been fully described in English, even by those who knew it and were in sympathy with it (like Lytton Strachey), so we must go back to our Sorbonne professor. Near the end of his careful enquiry into the technique of French classical plays M. Scherer has a page on this very point. He may seem to us to make high claims, but they form a suitable setting for a fresh approach:

The seventeenth-century understanding of the dramatic art brings with it a number of new techniques, of which it is not too much to say that they have made modern theatre possible. Every appearance of the central figure in the play is worked out and given its full effect. He is confronted, no longer just by ideas or by destiny, but by living people who are linked in a tight network of attitudes. The exposition is a part of the action. It was in seventeenth-century France that multiple turns of fortune were brought in, so similar to the very nature of theatre that they earned the name of 'coups de theatre'. It was in seventeenth-century France that the most complex plots were actually woven into a single action; henceforth a play did not merely tell a story, it had a subject. In the same period a way was found, not without many failures, of imposing strict limits on both the time duration and location of the play, and thereby of attaining an 'optic' natural to the theatre, thus setting it entirely apart from the novel, which allows of, and even welcomes, variety of both time and place. The denouement of a classical drama achieves the paradox of being at once a necessary and an unexpected outcome of the action. . . . In seventeenth-century France an attempt was made to attain that final perfection of literature, as Mallarmé was to call it, the elimination of chance, each entrance and exit being for a reason, each action down to the smallest details being governed by likelihood, and both credible and necessary. In short, it was at that time that men brought to the theatrical art all the ornaments of good writing, poetry, rhetoric, style, at times, indeed, with excessive abundance. It was in France that writers made of the theatre their main or sole means of expression, so that the result on the stage was both first-class drama and an authentic expression of the national genius. It will be agreed that these innovations have been of crucial importance in the general development of literature, and that therefore the creation of a classical form of the dramatic art in France must be seen as a decisive stage in the evolution of civilization.

(SCHERER, op. cit., p. 434)

Study of such a passage allows us to understand both why the French think so highly of their classical drama, and why foreigners like ourselves find it so hard to see their plays as they do. For example, how many of us take a play as a story, in which things happen and at the end of which conflicts are resolved? M. Scherer takes the very different view that a play is a study, in which the author plots the speeches, the entrances, the exits, with a definite end in view. That end is the full illumination of a subject, jealousy maybe or a power complex. They are, of course, plays with plots and characters as well, but neither plot nor psychology seems in classical drama to be primary. They are still what Aristotle said plays should be: they represent (literally re-present) an action. But close study of them reveals that they represent the physical aspects of an action badly, or not at all. They concentrate on the mental and poetic implications, so much so, indeed, that we can watch the great French classical authors neglecting plots which would have pleased Elizabethans, and going out of their way apparently to make five entire acts out of a plot as thin as that of *Bérénice* or *Le Malade Imaginaire*. We may not, as English readers, like this way of drama. But we must admit that it allowed things to be suggested on the stage which could not be said in any other way.

2
The Search for a Form

A FIRST question in historical science is to ask where phenomena
come from. The origins of French classical drama have not been
clearly set out, and no textbook gives the agreed answer. The usual
answer is that the form perfected in the seventeenth century was
little more than a hundred years old, and that it started as a revival
of interest in Seneca on the part of Renaissance poets. Gustave
Lanson could even pinpoint the starting-point and assign it to the
right poet. 'La *Cléopâtre* de Jodelle fonde la tragédie et le théâtre
moderne en France' (*Esquisse d'une histoire de la tragédie française*
(1927), p. 8). Many nineteenth-century assumptions lie hidden
beneath the verb *fondre*. The impetus given by the Pléiade to a
revival of Senecan drama is clear. A German scholar, however, takes
us much further back, to manuscripts of the fourteenth century,
more than twenty in number, of a certain *Albertini Musati
Tragoedia Eccerinis*. The curious thing about this dramatic presentation of the deeds and death of Attila, the Scourge of God, is
that it is not Senecan in spirit, although it has many formal features
(such as five acts, verse, chorus, etc.) in common. It is difficult to be
precise, let alone dogmatic, in a field where so little has survived,
but the studies of Wilhelm Cloetta leave us with the impression
that, well in advance of the age of printing, certain monks—
Mussato, Loschi, Corraro—suggested to their contemporaries a new
kind of drama, a drama using Senecan means, without the Senecan
fatalism or moralizing, a drama that should be not so much an
action as a poem, presenting a spectacle less pitiful than impressive.

Cloetta quotes at length from a Latin letter of Mussato enforcing these points. In particular, '. . . the deeds of princes are the matter of tragedy, and the noble names of kings, at a time when sudden crash overwhelms stricken houses. The terrifying lightning darts to the topmost towers and spares the hut of the humble man. In the verse of tragedy the sorrow of the great is sung and the noble song can only concern noble persons' (W. Cloetta, *Die Anfänge der Renaissancetragödie* (1892), p. 32).

There is nothing specifically Senecan about this view of tragedy, and it could apply to many of the plays of Racine. To call French classical tragedy Senecan in origin is to overlook some of its poetic features and to exaggerate the rhetoric which undoubtedly was also present. It is curious, and to my mind instructive, to find in monastery plays (of which no performance is known and which seem to Cloetta to have been written to be read), three hundred years before Racine, the urge to make noble words about great misfortunes. French tragedy at its best, says Thierry Maulnier, is comparable to a religious rite, an incantation, in which words are found which suggest calamity, despair, horror, but, at the same time, and by virtue of their poetic dignity, triumph, endurance, heroism in the human spirit. This ambivalence of language, which may be seen as a power to convey what Baudelaire would call action and dream in a single utterance, is a glory of French tragedy, and it is presumptuous to date its beginning. Our evidence is restricted to cases where manuscripts were widely circulated or to the ubiquity of the printed book. But who is to say that hearers of Abelard and Albert the Great and Grosseteste, and of a certain Nicholas Trivet who lectured on Seneca in fourteenth-century Oxford, did not have visions of a new art, which might celebrate in words the fears and the hopes of mankind? This would be an ideal beginning for classical drama, and it may not be so far from the fact. Let us put beside it the perfect achievement, by one of the great tragic poets of the world, strengthened as he was by a long tradition of rhetoric and gifted with the grace of poetry:

The tremendous role of Phèdre—which, as the final touchstone of great acting, holds the same place on the French stage as that of Hamlet on the English—dominates the piece, rising in intensity as act follows act, and 'horror on horror's head accumulates'. Here, too, Racine has poured out all the wealth of his poetic powers. He has performed the last miracle, and infused into the ordered ease of the Alexandrine a strange sense of brooding mystery and indefinable terror and the awful approaches of fate. The splendour of the verse reaches its height in the fourth act, when the ruined queen, at the culmination of her passion, her remorse and her despair, sees in a vision Hell opening to receive her, and the appalling shade of her father Minos dispensing his unutterable doom. The creator of this magnificent passage, in which the imaginative grandeur of the loftiest poetry and the supreme force of dramatic emotion are mingled in a perfect whole, has the right to walk beside Sophocles in the high places of eternity.

(L. STRACHEY, *Landmarks in French Literature* (1912), OPUS edn., p. 55)

Since in art it is true that 'in my end is my beginning', we may discern a connection between an apparently faltering beginning in a monastery and the supreme technical achievement of a classical dramatist. In somewhat the same sense, both are classical, and the design of Mussato finds full expression in Racine.

The intervening steps are doubtful, but we may accept that printing brought increased interest in Seneca and in his greater forerunners. The first decades of the sixteenth century saw Latin editions of Terence, Seneca, and Euripides, Latin translations of the *Hecuba* and *Iphigenia* by Erasmus, Italian and French versions of Greek plays, and (as a sort of culmination) the attempt by a Pléiade poet to imagine and express in French similar tragic attitudes. Jodelle's *Cléopâtre captive* is not a masterpiece, and has probably excited few readers since the sixteenth century, but it deserves, as Lanson said, to be called a starting point. I am not myself convinced by the generality of scholars that the classical theatre in France can be said with any accuracy to begin with the two plays of Jodelle (*Cléopâtre*, 1552; *Didon,* 1553). This Pléiade attempt at serious drama was, of course, in sharp contrast to what was supplied at the only serious Paris theatre, the Hôtel de Bourgogne, which until the edict of 1548, and possibly longer, purveyed the old-fashioned mystery plays, moralities, *soties*, and the like. Jodelle may have had in mind the sort of dramatic emotion which Racine was later to evoke. But he neither invented a new kind of play, nor offered a new version of Seneca. The surviving manuscripts studied by

Cloetta satisfy me that serious and repeated efforts were made in the monasteries to create a new kind of tragedy, which would be an impressive celebration of the inconstancy of fortune coupled with the human answer to disaster. These efforts are not mere Senecan imitation, and they are found two hundred years before Jodelle.

With these reservations I would agree that the Pléiade attempt to revive serious drama may be called a starting-point. But when we ask what was started we enter a field of interesting speculation and scanty information. In his epistle to the King, Jodelle asked leave to present

> une Tragédie
> Qui d'une voix plaintive et hardie
> Te représente un Romain, Marc Antoine
> Et Cléopâtre, Egyptienne Roine . . .

This seems to be something different from the 'noble song' of Mussato. It is nearer to the declamation of Seneca. The play opens with what is recognizably a 'voix plaintive' by the Shade of Antony, 150 lines of feminine Alexandrines, followed by a dozen single-line interchanges between Cleopatra and her ladies, thus:

> O Dieux, à quel malheur m'avez-vous alléchée?
> —O Dieux, ne sera point votre plainte étanchée?

The search for a form is clear. Should we go far wrong in supposing that the sort of pleasure designed, and conveyed, was that T. S. Eliot has described as 'unacted drama . . . at one remove from reality', in which 'characters behave like members of a minstrel troupe sitting in a semi-circle, rising in turn each to do his number'? (Introduction to *Newton's Tenne Tragedies of Seneca* (1927), pp. viii, x). The perils of such drama are obvious: lack of action, over-use of *sentences* and moral platitudes, rhetoric. But the Renaissance poets had no choice, maybe, other than the rough horseplay of the fairground and formal declamation. And, as Eliot goes on to ask, 'Certainly, it is all rhetorical, but if it had not been rhetorical, would it have been anything? . . . without bombast we should not have had *King Lear*.'

There is plenty of evidence that this new kind of play was

appreciated: it was played before the King; great lords gave their houses for private recitals; poets praised it in verse; actors made the most of royal costumes. More important, contemporaries tried their hand at evoking poetic figures of myth and history. Jacques Grévin, after paying tribute to his contemporary Jodelle for having had the idea of copying the tragic verses of antiquity, and 'pour les replanter en France', says that he had in so doing opened the way back to the Greek poets 'Aeschyle, Sophocle et Euripide, que nous osons à bon droit nommer la fontaine de laquelle tous les bons poètes Tragiques ont bu'; this was prefaced to a tragedy on Caesar, opening with a monologue presenting something more sophisticated and more modern than the famous conqueror

> César, non plus César, mais esclave de crainte,
> Vainqueur, non plus vainqueur, mais serf qui porte empreinte
> La honte sur le front.

Yet another contemporary defined the new style of play in a Preface to his play on the Biblical figure of Saul:

Tragedy therefore is a form and kind of poetry which is not for all comers, but which aims at the utmost elegance, beauty and perfection. Its true matter is the lamentable fall of great lords, the faithlessness of Fortune, great disasters such as exile, war, plague, poverty, woe, not at all those things which happen in the daily course of nature, such as natural death, being killed by one's enemy, legally sentenced to die for crimes committed, for all that would not be likely to provoke emotion, to bring tears to the eye. The true and sole aim of tragedy is emotion which will touch the heart of all present . . .

Now it is the great thing in tragedy to have the art of so arranging, constructing and linking its effects so that it alters and directs at will the mind of those who hear, and that it make them spectators of joy turned to sadness or of the reverse, as happens in real life.

(J. DE LA TAILLE, *De l'Art de la tragédie*, ed. F. West (1939), pp. 24, 26)

There is no need to speak of failures in our estimate of these experiments. They were probably both exciting and rewarding to their authors, to those who were fortunate enough to see performances in a college or great house, to readers whom they stimulated to read ancient drama and who provoked scholars to fresh commentaries, Scaliger (1566) for instance, and Castelvetro (1572). They

created for many lovers of literature what a modern scholar has
called a double oasis in the harsh reality of Renaissance life: 'The
times were harsh, rough and pitiless. Garnier's tragedy mirrors
these hard features but provides a double oasis of reflexion and of
weeping. There is much weeping in the theatre because there is
little but fighting, killing and dying in the street' (J. Vier, *Histoire
de la littérature française* (1959), i. 157).

It was in fact Robert Garnier, a Paris lawyer, who discovered a
tragic style and sense of dramatic composition which could clothe
the dry bones of Jodelle's lamentations. No wonder there has been
talk of pre-classicism, for he comes near to the classical dramatists
of the following century in several ways. We may note how he
recovers the tragic interest of the Greeks in the great subjects (the
Trojan Women, Hippolytus, and in great people like Mark Antony
and Portia. Yet the new tragic form was elastic enough to admit
of a play on a contemporary figure, as Montchrétien showed when
he made Mary Queen of Scots into a tragic heroine. Those of us
who study the subject have not perhaps made enough of the outstanding fact that the tragic figures evoked in this Pléiade revival
are not different in kind from the protagonists of Corneille and
Racine. And there is nothing exclusively French in this. Queen
Sophonisba (and her tragic choice of love or death) is treated by
Trissino in 1514, and by French dramatic poets in 1601 (Montreux),
in 1632 (Mairet), and in 1660 (Corneille). Cleopatra, Hippolytus,
Dido, Medea . . . these seem to attract Renaissance poets and
classical poets in equal measure. Is it any wonder that scholars have
concluded that Renaissance drama was a foretaste, a first shot, a
prelude, to classical drama, and that the former failed through lack
of funds and theatres and public, while the latter, thanks chiefly to
Richelieu, fostered the conditions which made it lucrative to be an
author, and still more an actor? All such views received a grave
rebuke from Gustave Lanson in his Columbia lectures of 1916,
notable not only for their clarity but for the fact that then for the
first time a Sorbonne scholar expounded to an American university
audience the complexities of French classical literature: 'Erreur de
considérer la tragédie de la Renaissance comme une tragédie
classique mal faite . . . n'ayant besoin que d'être améliorée' (Lanson,

op. cit., p. 16). But what the professor rebuked as error is still, I would think, the point of view of most students of the subject. Consider this from a recent (and stimulating) presentation; the play referred to is Grévin's *César*:

> Clearly, the action proper is confined to little: the indecisions of Caesar in the third Act. All the rest of the play is given up to political eloquence or to the pathetic lamentation of Calpurnia. But Grevin has made some effort to appeal to our senses: the horrid dream of Calpurnia, the account of Caesar's end, are highly coloured; the tragedy over, our eyes may feed if not on the corpse at least on the bloodstained toga displayed by Mark Antony to the soldiers.
>
> (J. MOREL, *La Tragédie* (1964), p. 14)

Such a passage as this shows, I believe, how we study Renaissance drama in order to remark those signs of incipient action and of illusion which show, as we say, that these early efforts are 'on the way' to the achievement of real tragic power, of the sort of power that Sophocles and Shakespeare and Corneille exert in and through the theatre. But it may be that such power was not consciously aimed at by Renaissance poets. Their work suggests something else; one might call it study-drama, or radio drama, where the actual illusion is of the barest—it may be a costume, a name, a reminder of famous happenings. The verse form, the stylized attitudes, and the wit, appear to suggest something like study of a passion, or a dilemma, a suggestion of reaction (not action) to events which suddenly provoke surprise or astonishment. Renaissance drama is often little more than meditation on suffering. Why should it be more? It aims at the pathetic, rather than what we take to be truly tragic. But this is not failure; it is search for a form.

Nor is it just a poetic meditation. It has an audience in mind; it aims to sketch, for hearers and spectators, a mood. The point comes out in a Preface to a Huguenot drama on David:

> Ici je représente, à l'ancienne mode,
> Quelques tragiques traits, lesquels je forme, autant
> Que la chose de soi me le va permettant.
> Parquoy si point ne sont agréables mes carmes

Aux esprits désireux des passions et larmes
Que peuvent exprimer les autres écrivains
Traitant sujets pour eux et profanes et vains,
Je les laisse admirer d'iceux la libre course
Qui déguise l'histoire et la vérité, pour ce
Que leur loi le permet.

(H. W. LAWTON, *Handbook to French Renaissance Drama* (1949), p. 68)

An interesting recent study on Castelvetro suggests, not only why
this Italian commentator of Aristotle achieved such notoriety, but
how it was that the new departure, far from lacking the dramatic
sense, discovered a new kind of dramatic pleasure. This cultivation
of what Desmasures called 'quelques tragiques traits' allowed the
poet to concentrate on the essence of a mood, to escape from con-
tinuity and sequence, such as the epic and the tale enforced, to
consider a situation in itself. Hence a quite new stress on concentration. Castelvetro puts it thus: '. . . tragedy must have as its subject
an action accomplished in a small area of place and in a small space
of time, that is, in that place and in that time where and when the
actors remain engaged in acting, and not in any other place or in
any other time' (*apud* B. Weinberg, 'Castelvetro's Theory of Poetics'
in *Critics and Criticism* (1952); paperback edn. (1957), p. 161). This
might seem to be but one item in the long and pedantic debate on
the unities, which used to be thought an essential feature of classical
drama. So it is, but for our purpose it is something else, a sign of
the new conception of dramatic illusion. Much of Racine's poetry
depends on this. Where did he get it from?

We may never discover the real answer to such a question. The
new stress on unity and concentration of effect was revived in the
1630s, as everyone knows, was explained in various ways and enforced by theorists, but that is perhaps less important than its
increasing adoption in plays that proved successful, that satisfied
the demands of repeated performance, many of which in fact have
kept their dramatic power up to our own day. For such a scholar as
Carrington Lancaster, French Renaissance drama is interesting in
so far as it supplied situations taken up by later poets. He tells us so
often that Molière and Racine took this detail from that author that
we look at these so-called sources in reverse and judge them as

having been just good enough to satisfy the demands and needs of a great dramatist. I suggest that a less metallic view is possible and that in Renaissance drama we are confronted with the search for a form. Poets desire a form which shall supply what rough drama does not supply, material for meditation and for wonder on the mystery of things and of minds, on the reverses of fortune, on the scandal of unmerited disgrace or untimely death, on the risk involved in great choices. A suitable form for expression of such attitudes was not a gimmick or a fashion: it was the result of many years of experiment. An example of this in delicate hands, both of author and of critic, may be had by comparing, as Mme de Mourgues has recently done,* the treatment of the Hippolytus story in Seneca and in Garnier. The Frenchman seems to have been as sensitive to the peculiar tragic quality of the Latin play, as he was anxious to use its theme for his own quite different purposes. If the wrong standard be applied, such as that the characters should be realistic and convincing as people, both plays seem botched. If we watch the contrary poetic suggestions of the beauty of nature and youth, of the pitiless intrusion of disaster, then something new, something like classical drama, becomes available to us.

But what of classical comedy? That is a different story altogether. The very nature of comedy would seem to resist classical treatment. Comedy deals, as all know, with the everyday, with the ordinary, which in fact means the particular, with prose rather than verse. The situation facing the young Pléiade poets in 1550 was that in both tragic and comic modes there was in France a long and rich tradition, but the *mystère* and the farce tended to be subject to popular appeal, hence to prefer the rough and the rowdy to the reflective, the moral, and the elegant. There was room, they thought, for experiments in a new comic mode, which would present ordinary life with something of the selectivity and concentration of the new tragedy. 'Comedy', says Lawton, 'portrayed the amorous complications in the lives of ordinary citizens; its beginnings were entangled and uneasy, its end joyful' (*Handbook*, p. xix). Grévin, in the *Brief Discours* already quoted, defines comedy as 'a

---

* In *The French Renaissance and its Heritage: Essays Presented to Alan Boase* (1968), pp. 191–202.

fictional discourse, approaching the truth, which contains various ways of life among middle-class citizens, and by means of which we may learn what is useful in life and what one should avoid, judging by the good fortune or misfortune of other people'. The same document quotes Andronicus' definition of comedy: 'le miroir de la vie journalière'.

Here we come upon a new difficulty which besets classical drama from the start. Since drama is a social art, the poet has a duty to society: his play must not be immoral, it must indeed be useful. From this it was a short step to saying that both comedy and tragedy must teach virtue. This is found until the late eighteenth century. Molière justified *Tartuffe* on the ground that it was an attack on vice. Whether authors or audiences believed in this therapeutic value of the theatre, nobody has ever found out. Clearly the matter of drama was not in general edifying. The story of Oedipus or Medea or Cleopatra is not morally improving. The matter of most comedies was nearer to nature than to virtue. Drama has always had to struggle, as it still does, against the moralist. The power of the Church over public morality was very great until mid-eighteenth century, and it was liable to be exerted against most forms of drama. Acting was an impious profession: no actor received Christian burial unless he renounced his sinful life. Bossuet probably spoke for many religious directors of conscience when he argued that the appeal of drama was to nature, to pleasure, even to licence. The better the play the more skilfully was the audience persuaded to sympathize with youth against age, with vice against authority. When we remember that even in the late eighteenth century Schiller had to construct a case in favour of the theatre as a moral institution, we can see why plays had to be 'improving'. According to Dickens even the Veneerings had to avoid mention of anything 'which might bring a blush to the cheek of the young person'.

Comedy is more open to the charge of immorality than tragedy, which may explain why learned comedy is so often dull and moralizing. Mr Lawton tells us what happened:

The emphasis on the moral and didactic aspect of the theatre led to the use and abuse of moral 'sentences' and maxims. Terence's comedies were a mine of these commonplaces, which were stuffed into French comedies

. . . what may appear to us the most immoral play is full of such moral quotations from one or other of the ancient writers, and the maxims are often brought into prominence by their enclosure in quotation marks.

A useful way out of their difficulties was offered to French poets by the flourishing comedies of a learned kind in Italy, which tended to present an imbroglio or complicated system of disguise; the course of the play made things plain and allowed characters to appear as themselves. Strangely enough, these foreign importations brought French comedy nearer to what we now regard as the French tradition of the rogue, to be realized in Mascarille, Scapin, and Figaro. One Renaissance theorist, indeed, sees the matter of comedy as consisting chiefly of deception: '[Comic] material as Plautus and Donatus understand it . . . consists of fraud and trickery, of the young against the old, of servants' tricks, of stolen virgins . . . of rogues' encounters and of the swindling of servants. We are shown no serious people, just old men, women, chamberers, bakers, weavers, guild members, captains, dandies, and the like.' (P. de Laudun Daigaliers, *apud* Lawton, op. cit., p. 91).

While we may no longer say that these Renaissance experiments 'led to' classical comedy, we are entitled to admire and respect the attempt to provide a poetic kind of comedy, which should rise above vulgarity (was this not the Pléiade claim in all kinds of writing?), and which curiously explored comic motifs used by later and finer dramatists. Does any comic theme go deeper than disguise? La Rochefoucauld was to sum up his age in the phrase: 'le monde est composé de mines', and Molière's plays provide a series of illustrations of the ways in which 'le réel' lies hidden behind polite speech and good manners. Once again, as in the new tragedy, have not the advocates of a new comedy built better than they knew, whether their work was actually known to Molière or not? It is not often noted that all these experiments took place within a sick and divided society, which for twenty years and more was to be torn by civil war. It was only with Henri IV that the return of peace and leisure allowed much interest to be taken in such things as dramatic entertainment. Yet it seems that public concern for drama was on the increase even before the end of the century. Many scraps of evidence all point in the same direction. We read for example of the arrival

B

in Bordeaux in 1592 of an accomplished actor: 'It was in that year that Valeran, a distinguished French actor, came to Bordeaux, where he performed many tragedies and farces, much applauded by the public.' His wife seems to have caused comment also, since she played feminine roles (instead of the men who were expected to play them): 'she would never play any role in a farce, but only in tragedy or tragicomedy those parts which were suitable for her sex. This caused the rumour in Bordeaux that she was really a well-born girl from Paris.'

Things were changing too at the single established theatre of Paris, the Hôtel de Bourgogne:

The theatre at the Hôtel de Bourgogne, established in 1548, was at the first confined to plays put on by the Confrères de la Passion. Since they did not prosper, a company of professional players was hired by them in 1578 to play in their stead, but it would seem that the repertoire was not much different and the management would not give up any but temporary control. Indeed, they took back their stage, but not for long, and never returned. . . . From 1598 their role was confined to letting out their premises, to levying a tax on all Paris playing, and to litigation against those who claimed to be unaware of the privileged position of the Hôtel.

(E. RIGAL, *Le Théatre français avant la période classique* (1901), p. 79)

The story of what happened to this famous theatre is best read in H. C. Lancaster's *History of French Dramatic Literature in the Seventeenth Century* (1942). The company known as the Comédiens du Roi were, it appears, fined in 1622 for playing elsewhere than in the Hôtel, and from 1629 onwards became its permanent tenants. But troupes of French actors are traced in the Netherlands and England, of Italian actors in Paris. The Hôtel was more than once leased to the players of the Prince of Orange, among whom the famous name of Mondory first occurs. It seems a far cry from occasional leasing of this or that tennis court to the establishment of a second, and by mid century of a third, permanent theatre in Paris, but these bare facts must be put back, as Lancaster's *History* enables us to do, into a social context in which interest in the drama seems to be increasing, especially among the upper class. Entertainments are given, one of the most splendid that in late December 1629, when Richelieu 'fit un superbe festin au Roi et aux Reines, avec comédies, ballets et musiques excellentes'. French taste hardly varied from this pattern throughout the Splendid Century, as Louis XIV's reign has been called. Entertainment seems to have been understood at Court and in great houses as involving both dance and music. Such a play as *Le Bourgeois Gentilhomme* is described in the original programme as one item in a series of mostly musical pieces. By the end of his career Molière seems indeed to have had to yield to the popularity of Lulli and the operetta.

Professional actors, regular performance . . . but of what? The early years of the century seem to show a new kind of play, in which the content itself is sensational; adventure, novelty, incident seem to be required. One title among many: 'Comédie admirable intitulée la merveille, où l'on voit comment un Capitaine François, esclave du Soldan d'Egypte, transporté de son bon sens, se donne au diable pour s'affranchir de servitude, lequel il trompe mesme subtillement tant qu'il fut contraint lui rendre son obligation.' Such was the Faustian entertainment offered to citizens of Rouen in 1612 (Lancaster, *History*. I. i. 138).

Some remarkable developments of popular comedy took place on the Pont Neuf in Paris in the early 1620s, invented by two brothers Girard, one of whom took the stage name of Tabarin. It seems to have been a mixture of farce, quips, dialogue and horseplay, but seasoned with obscenity and a new kind of wit. Perhaps an example may still suggest the novelty. Here is No. 3 of a series of 'rencontres, questions, demandes et autres oeuvres tabariniques', published in 1622 and reprinted fifteen times by 1664. The question raised is this: ' Chercher ce qu'on ne veut pas trouver'.

Tabarin: Notre maître, me répondez-vous bien à ce que je vous vais demander?

Le Maître: Je ne sais pas, Tabarin. Tu as aucunefois des questions si éloignées de raison que les plus subtils se trouveraient bien empêchés d'en sortir.

Tabarin: C'est la vérité, j'ai étudié, oui; o diable, je sais du latin; je suis bon astrologue, je prévois le passé; quand il n'y a personne au logis je conclus nécessairement que le maître et les servi-

> teurs sont dehors. Dites-moi cependant, comment se peut-il
> faire qu'un homme aille cherchant ce qu'il ne veut pas
> trouver?

Le Maître: Cela ne se peut faire, Tabarin, à tout le moins d'un homme
sensé et qui a du jugement; car ce serait lutter contre la raison
même, et être privé de cette lumière naturelle de l'intellect, et
en ceci celui qui le chercherait se contrarierait soi-même, et
serait susceptible de deux formes contraires, qui, selon les
philosophes, ne se retrouvent jamais en un même sujet.*

At times one has the feeling of an exercise in wit not far from
Molière. Here is Tabarin's pre-view, so to say, of Monsieur Jourdain.
'Question 29: En quoi consiste la noblesse?'

Tabarin: Quand je considère mon extraction et l'origine de mes aïeux,
il me prend un désir de savoir en quoi consiste d'être noble.
Le Maître: On peut être noble en trois façons . . . [a page of elaboration].
Tabarin: S'il est vrai ce que vous venez de dire, je veux désormais porter
l'épée, car je suis gentilhomme.
Le Maître: Allez, gros nigaud, gros villageois que vous êtes. Voilà pas un
brave gentilhomme.
Tabarin: Je soutiens que je suis noble, par sang, mérites, lettres (apportées
par le facteur).*

        (*Les Oeuvres de Tabarin*, ed. G. d'Harmonville (1858), pp. 15, 48)

A similar change in taste overcame the repertory of regular plays.
Only two pastorals are known before Henri IV, no less than twenty
were put on during his reign. The success of l'*Astrée* was such
that it was adapted for many theatrical performances. Ariosto and
Tasso served in the same way as source material. Analysing all the
extant plays before 1610, Lancaster finds 'a marked tendency to have
the action, both physical and psychological, take place before our
eyes, thus shifting the emphasis from lamentation to action'. At such
a moment, as if to satisfy, and possibly also to create, the new
demand, appears the strange figure of Alexandre Hardy, a sort of
French Lope da Vega, twenty-four of whose reputed 600 plays
were published (this in itself a new departure) before 1628. Georges

---

* For translation see end of chapter, p. 28.

Scudéry, in a play about players (*La Comédie des Comédiens*) in 1635, gave him this epitaph:

He had enormous talent, and abundant facility of invention. . . . It is indeed to him alone that goes the glory of having raised the reputation of the theatre in France, which for long had been at a low ebb. He was a man of both invention and principle, and whatever his detractors may say, he was clearly a great man, and if he had written for pleasure as well as for duty, his works would have been incomparable. Yet he was out of pocket, like others of his trade.

(Lancaster, II. i. 41)

This was the man who presented to the new type of French play-goer such figures as Coriolanus, Herod and Mariamne, Achilles, Alexander, Timoclea, Cornelia. It was probably his example that encouraged Corneille's contemporary Tristan to treat the Mariamne theme, with a success that paralleled that of *Le Cid*. It is not a theme that would appeal because of its incident so much as a clash of temperament, of a subtlety that tempted Hebbel in the mid-nineteenth century. To speak only of Hardy is perhaps less than fair to new talent, which is discernible in several places and cases.

The years that precede Richelieu's return to power mark the entrance of poets into the growing company of dramatists and with them the emphasis shifts from plot to the emotions of the characters, the versification becomes more correct, and one finds more frequently plays that show no indecency. . . . Racan and Theophile were not only among the three or four leading poets of the day, but they were also nobles well known at court. If they wrote plays for professional actors, no other persons of good birth need hesitate to do so. Moreover their plays, the *Bergeries* and *Pyrame*, are the first of the century to acquire permanent fame.

(Lancaster, II. i. 156)

Both these popular plays illustrate the variety in subject and character that the new public seems to have demanded. In the *Bergeries* (?1620) we have the usual pastoral material, mostly taken from Guarini, with satyr, magician, and crossed lovers. *Pyrame*, probably a little later than the *Bergeries*, no doubt increased its appeal by being the work of the noted free-thinker Théophile de Viau. Georges Scudéry in 1635 said that everybody interested in the stage still knew it by heart. Boileau's attack on the lines about a dagger blushing with bloodstains is also an indirect compliment to its enduring appeal.

In any evolution of taste such as the one we are here tracing, it is difficult to know whether to speak of general tendencies or of personal forces. Rigal speaks of Hardy as having rescued the cause of serious drama in France. Lancaster, going over the ground more carefully, came to the view that 'French classical tragedy might have developed as it did, had Hardy never existed' (Lancaster, i. 23). The evidence seems to me such as to encourage speculation in both directions. For similar doubts arise concerning the great figure of Richelieu. That he deliberately and successfully encouraged theatrical production in Paris is very clear. His edict of 1641, ensuring good lighting and policing of theatre premises, is but one of many cases of personal intervention. He built a hall for plays; he encouraged authors, he even wrote for the theatre, and contemporaries speak with one voice as to his decisive influence. Tallemant for example: 'La comédie n'a été en honneur que depuis que le cardinal de Richelieu en a pris soin . . . avant cela les honnêtes femmes n'y allaient point.' I do not think Lancaster's work has affected the validity of Rigal's judgement: 'It was public taste that had altered, far more than the capacity of actors or the kind of play. At first gradually, then ever more speedily, and finally very swiftly under the influence of Richelieu, taste had changed, farce was thought less of, real drama was supplanting it' (op. cit., pp. 213, 188).

We must not imagine rough entertainment giving place to entire elegance. A serious play had always to be accompanied on the bill by a farce, or to finish with a topical (and often obscene) *chanson*. Much of the dramatic content of plays was not dramatic at all, but episodic, romanesque, topical, scurrilous. The autopsy of this production is available in the most meticulous of literary histories, that of Professor Lancaster, whose volumes analyse for us the content of every extant play. Even from so complete a survey conclusions are not easy to draw. If we remember that most Parisians never saw a play, that the Hôtel de Bourgogne admitted less than 500 people at a time, then what validity have our assumptions drawn from the mass of ephemeral plots and bombast that Mr Lancaster has exhumed? Perhaps this much, that French taste for polite entertainment admitted serious drama in both the tragic and the comic mode, in profusion and of great variety. As we should expect, it was written and acted for the taste of the moment. Its appeal did not last, save in the tradition it helped to form. Most of it shows no sign of that search for a poetic form which the Pléiade tried to satisfy. There is no care any more for the 'noble song' of tragedy, no observance of the conventions of Seneca. There is perhaps something more important, the emergence of a taste for, and a skill in supplying, *dramatic* material, that is material that conveys suspense, heightened interest, a problem or a conflict moving towards an end that shall be followed and desired and enjoyed by an audience. No matter how undiscriminating that audience was: it would not stand for mere lamentation, or for rhetoric that had no dramatic function. And from what came afterwards we may suppose that such audiences included a critical element, people who were later to insist on regular and stylized drama, on plays of maximum concentration, of single appeal, in a dramatic form that should convey the comic or the tragic but not both at once, in verse that allowed them to glimpse their own dilemmas while they watched those of ancient or great persons. By a roundabout and apparently haphazard process these years without masterworks seem to supply what Renaissance experiments lacked, an interest in gesture and word which would hold the attention of a modern audience. It was a basis on which skilful artists might create a classical play.

Page 24, note *

Master, will you give a serious answer to what I shall ask you?

— I don't know, Tabarin. You often ask questions so devoid of reason that the cleverest man could not find an answer.

— True, for I have studied, I know Latin, the devil I do, I am a sound astrologer, I foresee the past. If there is nobody at home I draw the conclusion that both master and servants are out. But tell me: how can a man go about seeking what he does not wish to find?

— That cannot be, Tabarin, at least not in the case of a man of sense and judgement, for that would be to resist reason itself, and to forego that natural light of our intellect; to seek to do that would be to go against oneself, and to take on two forms at variance, which according to the philosophers is beyond the power of one man.

*   *   *

When I consider the history of my family and the origins of my forebears, I have a wish to know wherein nobility consists.

— There are three ways of being noble. . . .

— If what you say is true I wish to bear the sword henceforth, for I am a gentleman.

— Go on, you fat old country numbskull. What a fine gentleman you would make.

— I maintain I am noble, first by descent, then by noble qualities, also by letters (posted rather than patent). . . .

3
The Thirties

In 1660 Pierre Corneille, enjoying a great reputation as a playwright, but scenting hostility, which had suddenly become vocal in
the person of one Hedelin, Abbé d'Aubignac, republished his entire
dramatic work, attaching an *Examen* to each play. What he there
says about his first comedy, *Mélite* (1629 or 1630), makes it a valuable document for our present purpose. It is so, not so much for
facts and dates, for thirty years may have blurred his recollection,
but for the spirit in which so practised a practitioner of the stage
looked back, on his own beginnings and on a notable change in
public taste:

This was my first play, and it shows no effort to keep within the
Rules, because I did not then know of their existence. My sole guide
was a modicum of common sense, my sole example the plays of the late
M. Hardy, a writer more prolific than elegant, and of certain young
dramatists, achieving public notice, who cared for regularity no more
than he did. The success of the play was a surprise. It established a new
troop of actors in Paris, even though the one already there was both
experienced and anxious to keep its monopoly. The play was as well spoken
of as any, and procured me introductions at Court.

The novelty of this type of comedy, unknown in other languages, and
its homely style, describing how elegant folk actually converse, were no
doubt the reason for its surprisingly good reception and the fuss that it
caused. It was the first play to cause laughter without the aid of stock
buffoons, like the Sponger, the Captain, the Doctor. It did this by means
of the jocular tone of well-bred people, of a better class than are found in
Plautus and Terence, who only deal in tradesmen. Yet in spite of all this,

I must confess that my public was very easy to please in approving a play of such unconvincing structure.

(P. CORNEILLE, *Mélite*, ed. Roques & Lièvre (1950), p. 134)

Any preface is a suspect document, especially in a time of polemic, and if this one were by Racine we should have to be cautious about taking any of it at face value. But Corneille was a man of simpler make-up; he had a better case and was not surrounded by enemies. We know from other witnesses that many of his statements are true. Indeed, if they were not, they would have been refuted with joy by contemporaries for whom the notorious 'Querelle du Cid' had shown Corneille in a bad light. (I am here accepting M. Adam's view that the venom of that 'Querelle' was largely caused by Corneille himself, in particular by his vanity in the *Excuse à Ariste* and by his haste to publish his play before its first actors had made reasonable profits out of it.)

Corneille in this passage allows us a valuable glimpse into the state of mind of those who cared about drama in Paris around the year 1630. He suggests the existence of a public undisturbed by the Rules, but keen to welcome a play that was neither rough like the farce, nor complicated like many tragicomedies, a play which gave the enjoyment and the illusion of polite conversation, of light-hearted complications, between men about women, between women about men, and between the sexes about how much they might mean of what they said. To take one example for many, we find a sonnet scene which no doubt gave something of the same kind of pleasure as that in the *Misanthrope* was to do thirty-five years later:

> Ma soeur, un mot d'avis sur un méchant sonnet
> Que je viens de brouiller dedans mon cabinet. . . .
> — Tu l'as fait pour Eraste?
>   — Oui, j'ai dépeint sa flamme.
> — Comme tu la ressens peut-être dans ton ame?
> — Tu sais mieux qui je suis, et que ma libre humeur
> N'a de part en mes vers que celle de rimeur.
> — Pauvre frère, vois-tu, ton silence t'abuse,
> De la langue, ou des yeux, n'importe qui t'accuse. . . .

This is light stuff compared to Renaissance comedy. It must have conveyed, says Mario Roques, 'une fantaisie, une audace ignorante, une fraîcheur et même une verdeur, que le changement de goût de Corneille ou des goûts du public et l'observance de la mode ont éteints'. This change of taste springs to the eye if one compares the editions of 1633 and 1660: over 600 lines have been altered, in many cases by substitution of a more orthodox and conventional word such as *tromperie* for *piperie*, *hymenée* for *mariage*, *honteux* for *sale*. We may imagine, therefore, that the first audiences were given something more natural, more realistic than was later thought to be 'classical'. The simplified setting must have had an effect. The decorators' manual known as the *Mémoire de Mahelot* shows that until 1640 the authority of the medieval multiple *décor* was still binding, but in comedy Corneille supplied an action needing hardly any setting, and no change of scene. The light-hearted verse was much better served by the new single *décor* of Serlio and his Italian disciples. This showed a street, opposing rows of houses, and a distant perspective.

It is perhaps at this point that we face a difficulty peculiar to the study of drama. As André Gide said, in the opening words of a lecture of 1904: 'L'évolution de l'art dramatique est un sujet tout particulièrement difficile.' The point has already been made in these pages that a play is more than a printed text. It is realized only in the act of playing, by players trained in their art, before a public for whom (rather than for any body of readers) the play is meant. Study of dramatic texts is therefore insufficient if we wish really to understand drama. What lies behind the texts? Most books assume that drama is written, very much as poetry or fiction is written, by a poet, that is by someone comparable to a poet or novelist. But this is only part of the real story. Even Racine cannot have written his plays out of the blue. He had in mind the scene on which they would be staged, the people who would listen to them, and in particular the actors and actresses who would have to make them come alive, in that place and for that public. That penetrating woman Mme de Sévigné once said that he wrote with one actress in mind. If we believe her, we should have to read *Bajazet* and *Mithridate* with the part taken by Mlle Champmêlé as clue to the structure.

But a dramatic poet depends on material things, on the scenery and properties available to him. Considerable research has been done on such matters, and we now know much more about the conditions of the Paris seventeenth-century stage than was available to me as a student. Documents have been discovered, chiefly by Mme Deierkauf-Holsboer, giving details of properties and effects. Carrington Lancaster's edition of the *Mémoire de Mahelot* (1920), Mahelot's drawings of sets, Mr Kernodle's illustrations to his book (Chicago, 1944), M. Védier's researches as to the nature and role of the curtain (1955), and Professor Lawrenson's drawings and pictures in his book on *The French Stage in the Seventeenth Century* (1957) —these constitute in my view a body of evidence that makes the older views untenable, just as the influence of Serlio and the Italian decorators in 1630 made the multiple stage (inherited from the *mystères*) impracticable. It would seem that the painters of scenery (for lack of time) preferred to show a single view, perhaps with a *ferme*, or shutter, at the back of the stage to reveal a more intimate scene. To do this they took material lying to hand in the many sketches for triumphal arches needed by any city in order to welcome great persons. The *tableaux vivants* of street theatres would supply similar material (see the illustrations in Lawrenson, and his pp. 36–7). Such scenery would be made more interesting by a central perspective, the end of a street, gardens or trees, thus focusing rather than dispersing the gaze of spectators.

It is in this setting, perhaps, that we should think of the part played by the curtain, which (as we might expect) was used to open and to close the vista of illusion. 'Le théâtre s'ouvre', say stage directions. Fortunately, an extra number of the *Gazette* in 1650 was devoted to a description of Corneille's new-machine play *Andromède*. The description ends with this passage:

Then the curtain which had risen so smartly at the start of the play, and now fell with equal speed, shuts out the decor leaving the audience like the man who in sleep was transported full of delights, which when he had tasted and been returned to whence he came was in two minds as to where he was and whether waking or sleeping.

(Corneille, Œuvres, 'Les Grands Écrivains de la France', henceforth GE, v. 289)

The very confusion of the reporter's language suggests that the great thrill was the revelation of an enchanted land and its closure when the show was over. On the basis of such references M. Védier has cogently argued that seventeenth-century theatres used a curtain, when at all, for this purpose, and not to separate scenes. If this was the case, then we may be all wrong about the unity of place being 'imposed' by theorists. I think that M. Védier's argument deserves careful reading:

> The curtain at the front of the stage, as used in the sixteenth and seventeenth centuries, has nothing to do with dividing the play into Acts, and is far from being the means of showing changes of time and place as it does today. On the Italian stages of the sixteenth century its purpose is to reveal the décor to the audience. It is the means of that pictorial illusion we see in the plastic arts of the time: its particular service in both France and Italy is to act as seal and symbol of a single theatrical illusion, so often employed that it develops into an esthetic necessity, preventing the décor from being shut off between acts, and making any change of time and place seem improbable. It thus seals the victory of the Rules.
>
> (G. VEDIER: *Origine et évolution de la dramaturgie néo-classique* (1955), p. 35. Lancaster would agree with these statements: cf. Lancaster, I. ii. 714-17.)

It is one thing to see a play as a co-operative effort; it is quite another to discern who and what gave the impetus that made the play what it is. Was it the new generation of writers, who wrote plays for which traditional scenery was no longer adequate? Or did the impulse come from the actors, who asked for the speeches they liked, and the designers whose settings gave such pleasure that new plays had to be written for the new sets? Despite the flood of argument on these matters, I am unable to decide. We do not know enough to be dogmatic. I think that we do know enough to reject the notion that theorists forced new conceptions of drama on producers. Classical concentration, which after all is the principle behind the Rules, may well have come about almost unnoticed, as a result of various forces and persons co-operating to supply a new kind of entertainment. About this new sort of play we really know only two things. First, that it gave pleasure, that the new audiences liked concentration and simplification, no more, perhaps, but certainly no less than they liked incident and spectacle. Second, that it supplied a valid form for dramatists of outstanding abilities. Was it not the genius of Corneille and Molière and Racine that persuaded the French (and indeed European taste in general) that a classical play was the most effective kind of play? If so, one should probably add that their achievement is unthinkable apart from the tradition we are studying, since it fashioned for their benefit a form which was the condition of their writing.

It is also likely that to isolate Corneille from his colleagues is inaccurate. The books convey the impression that he was superior, even before 1640, to the other three or four writers of successful plays. This is hard to justify, even if we grant that Le Cid had a quite extraordinarily successful run. All that the actual evidence allows us to say is, not that his comedies were more comic or his tragedies more tragic than the rest, but that his keen sense of theatre and his technical virtuosity enabled him to renew his appeal and to keep his public, at first with a new kind of comedy, then with a tragicomedy, and finally with a series of Roman tragedies, which did in fact show a dramatic power of rare distinction. But until Le Cid none of his works seem in a different class from Mairet's Sylvie and Sophonisbe, or Tristan's Mariamne. We may think of him in fact as one of a gifted group, not as 'le grand Corneille'.

Let us remember that literature still depended on patronage, and that authors who became successful did so because they were favoured by the great rather than paid by the public. The Duc de Montmorenci, for example, seems to have appointed as his secretary at Chantilly a young man from Besançon, Jean Mairet, who in 1626 or thereabouts wrote (possibly as a domestic entertainment after a military campaign) a pastoral, Sylvie. Lancaster has shown how he made use of Théophile's Pyrame (Théophile was also employed by Montmorenci), of Racan's Bergeries, and of Italian pastorals. The verse, the tight structure, avoiding repetition and arranging surprises, caused it to be a selling hit, to the extent of being reprinted thirteen times in seven years. Thus encouraged, the young author attempted something more ambitious, still a pastoral but, as his preface says, written even more tightly, 'avec toutes les rigueurs que les Italiens ont accoutumé de pratiquer en cet agréable genre d'écrire, auquel il faut avouer que trois ou quatre des leurs ont divinement bien réussi' (Lancaster, I. ii. 376). We may note in passing that here, as often in dramatic history, French innovators have renewed their public by clever adaptation of foreign material. *Le Cid* and *Dom Juan* are two out of many cases that spring to mind. The next stage in the story concerns an actress. Tallemant, who made it his business to find out all he could about interesting people, has this passage about the wife of the actor Le Noir, who served in succession the players of the Prince of Orange, the new company at the Marais, and after 1634 the Hôtel de Bourgogne: 'This Le Noir girl was as pretty a morsel as you could find. The Comte de Belin, who employed Mairet, had plays written which gave her the chief role, for he was sweet on her and the troop profited from the fact' (Lancaster, ii. 744). Such may well be the background to one of the first French tragedies that we may call classical, on the subject of *La Sophonisbe*, which, as we have seen, had attracted an Italian dramatist as early as 1515, and was treated by no less than six French playwrights. For rhetorical and declamatory drama we can see that the theme was ideal: the queen who after her husband's death demands of Massinisse, the victorious general, that she be spared a Roman triumph. Their impossible love caused his, and finally her, suicide. Here seem to be all the ingredients: passion, peripety, preciosity, affectation, emotion. The verse form of the Alexandrine allows new and striking expression of attitudes, and attitudes that we recognize as having been imitated in the classical plays we know. Here we have a battle reported, and a final curse on Rome, as in *Horace*. We have the languorous figure of the captive queen, as in *Andromaque*. Racine surely recalled the lament of Sophonisbe:

Captive, abandonnée, au milieu des ennuis. (891)

Not only so, but the conceit of comparing the arrows of fate and the arrows of war, and the glances of the lady's eye:

Par vos regards, ces traits de lumière et de flamme,
Dont j'ai senti les coups au plus profond de l'âme;
Par ces noirs tyrans dont j'adore les loix,
Ces vainqueurs des vainqueurs, vos yeux maîtres des Rois.
(912-15)

Let us be sure that we do not apply the wrong standards of judgement here. The feelings expressed may seem unreasonable, excessive, we may think them 'theatrical'—but this is just what they were, this is why they gave pleasure. The task of the dramatist seems to have been to supply a framework, a backcloth akin to the actual décor, just sufficient to convey the illusion. For an unsophisticated public the voice of the actor did the rest.

As if inspired by Mairet's play, a contemporary in the service of Gaston d'Orléans, Tristan l'Hermite, wrote for the Marais in early 1636 a modern setting of the tragedy of Alexandre Hardy on *Mariamne*. The execution, the rhetoric, the concentration, were as brilliant as in *Sophonisbe*, with the added charm of an all-too-human theme. The poignant interest of a queen being treated as a chattel, and a conqueror being reduced to a slave, is exploited with great force by Tristan. As if trying to give his reader the impression of the first audience he added in the first edition a prose summary or argument before each Act. These summaries still convey, I think, some of the original force of the dramatic illusion:

Herod accuses Mariamne and produces before her the cupbearer who maintains that she intended to poison the king. Defending herself against this crime, she shows more courage than wit. Defying fate and death with the highminded courage of a great lady, she cannot avoid the tears of nature. . . . Herod, affected by her weeping, finds his love for her, driven out through the door of fear and anger, returning through that of pity. . . .

After the great storm, in which Mariamne wrecks her life, Herod recovers, comes to his senses, and has a horror of his cruelty. . . . At this point his violent spirit, which had always been attracted to the beautiful and chaste princess, is given up to grief, . . . appeals to the Jews, . . . is carried away by anger, . . . falls in a frenzy. . . . At the last his troubled mind argues his irreparable loss with profitless reasoning. . . .

(ed. Madeleine, pp. 62, 102)

Need we wonder that the fortunes of the Marais theatre were established by such a play, that good judges recalled, many years after, the acting of Mondory as a revelation, and a recovery of the ancient power of tragedy? A contemporary, Claveret, writes three or four years later: 'Avez-vous vu la *Mariane* et *Le Cid*? Il y a de ravissantes choses' (Bernardin, *Tristan*, p. 191, n.). This accords entirely with Rapin's reflexion, based no doubt on personal visits or those of an eyewitness: 'We have lately seen a rough outline of the kind of effects worked in the past by Tragedy. When Mondory played in the *Mariane* of Tristan at the Marais theatre, the people always came away in a mood of thought and reflexion, going over what they had just seen, and at the same time full of a great feeling of pleasure' (ed. Madeleine, p. xxiii).

The Jesuit father has perhaps come nearer than any modern scholar to the secret of the dramatic revival that we are here trying to appreciate. Tragedy, says Albert Camus, is a rare visitor to civilization. The visitation occurred without apparent cause in ancient Greece, in Elizabethan England, and surely also in Paris from 1630 to 1680. One has only to compare with the words just quoted the beautiful analysis of tragic pleasure composed by La Bruyère, quoted elsewhere in this book, to see how unjust it is to think of the 1630s as memorable because of *Le Cid*.

For it is in this context that *Le Cid* should be read and imagined: a context of intense dramatic experiment, a new theatre, a new company, a new type of play. Surely all these things inspired the writer of clever light pieces like *Mélite* to write for Mondory a play attractive in form, enthralling in interest, exploiting the pleasure of concentrated suspense, of finding grand words for great matters. The matter of *Le Cid* is epic in kind. In treating it Corneille addresses himself, as Marty-Laveaux put it, to 'la lutte du poème dramatique contre l'épopée'. One has only to read, in the original, or in the French summary (in GE edition, iii), Guillem de Castro's mammoth play 'en trois journées' to appreciate with what skill Corneille has picked out and filed down, so to say, the essential dramatic moments, leaving the rest aside. As Lancaster says: 'Corneille changed the work from a chronicle-play to the study of a definite problem, reduced the number of characters, analysed their states of mind, and gave to his play a unity that its Spanish predecessor was far from possessing' (op. cit., II. i. 125).

This is not the place to study afresh, after so many attempts by so many experts, the structure and content of *Le Cid*. Within our context it does represent the realization of a form after which so many dramatists had been seeking, in so many ways, for nearly a hundred years. The form is achieved by a playwright who was obviously a master craftsman. This is seen in the easy and masterly fusion of various elements: the idea of honour, the romanesque, the conflict of personalities, the psychological subtleties revealed by the verse form, the Alexandrine which can be as prosaic and informative as it can be rhythmical and suggestive. In a sense, Scudéry was not altogether wrong in asserting, in the heat of the famous *Querelle*, that 'le sujet ne vaut rien du tout'. One feels, as no doubt many of the first audience felt, that things are arranged, that life is not like this, that we are in the domain of fantasy, of make-believe. This is in fact the charm: problems are suggested, but never taken to the point of that realism which had made the success of Herod in Tristan's play. The moral of the fairy story hangs over these delightful interchanges. It is perhaps the perfection of tragicomedy.

Why then did Corneille insist on changing the title, in 1648, and calling his play a tragedy? We may have our differing views, but we can all see how Corneille developed his romanesque subject in such a manner as to approach the dignity of the tragic style. When he was engaged in replying to the attacks of D'Aubignac in 1660, he referred more than once to tragic situations in *Le Cid*. In the 1630s the notion of tragedy was not as clear-cut as it later became. It was, for example, quite compatible with a happy ending, as Corneille showed at the beginning of his 'Discours des trois unités': he makes the point that the unity of action of a comedy lies in unity of plot, in a tragedy in unity of peril: 'l'unité d'action consiste dans la comédie en l'unité d'intrigue, ou d'obstacle aux desseins des principaux acteurs, et en l'unité de péril dans la tragédie, soit que son héros y succombe, soit qu'il en sorte' (GE, i. 98).

The last words, not often remarked on, show that in Corneille's mind the distinguishing mark of a tragedy was not the way things worked out but the kind of danger that the actors incurred. In this sense certain lines of *Le Cid*, as Mondory declaimed them, must have conveyed that sense of loss, even of despair, of vain resistance to implacable circumstance, which the public had heard in

Mariamne and *Médée*. Consider this example from the famous stances which are the climax of the opening Act:

> Respecter un amour dont mon âme égarée
> Voit la perte assurée.
> N'écoutons plus ce penser suborneur
> Qui ne sert qu'à ma peine.
> Allons, mon bras, sauvons du moins l'honneur
> Puisqu'après tout il faut perdre Chimène.

It is of such lines that Corneille must have been thinking when, twenty-five years later, he claimed that in *Le Cid* he had attained the perfect form of tragedy: 'Établissons pour maxime que la perfection de la tragédie consiste bien à exciter de la pitié et de la crainte par le moyen d'un premier acteur, comme peut faire Rodrigue dans *Le Cid*, et Placide dans *Théodore*' (GE, i. 62). All this would seem to bear out the justice of Lanson's conclusion, 'c'est dans la tragi-comédie du Cid qu'il découvre la vraie tragédie' (*Corneille*, p. 52).

If the preceding points be sound, the question as to whether *Le Cid* is a tragedy is not only a wrong but a sterile question. We can see why Corneille called it a tragicomedy in 1637 and a tragedy in 1648: both descriptions fit. To see the play as a classical tragedy which is still impeded by foreign material of a romanesque kind is as unjust as to view it as a rollicking heroic play that should not be taken too seriously. As a play it disappoints only those who look in it for the sort of tragedy which Shakespeare and Racine and Ibsen supply. By comparison with them it is not inferior tragedy, but dramatic entertainment, containing elements of both tragedy and fantasy. The theory known as 'la distinction des genres' grew up in the wake of Racine; it should not be used as a measuring rod for Corneille or Molière. Corneille was, in fact, the sort of dramatic poet who was most happy in offering different kinds of entertainment. As Professor Yarrow puts it: 'Corneille does not make a clear-cut distinction between comedy and tragedy: his conception of tragedy embraces comedy as well. His characters, given to teasing and irony, fond of using familiar language, sometimes comic in their blunt outspokenness, their innuendos, their double-entendre, and the contrast between their words and their inmost thoughts, are human and natural' (*Corneille* (1963), p. 176).

In fact one sure way of sensing the novelty and the pleasure given by these classical plays of the 1630s is to take them (as the most intelligent contemporaries took them) as entertainment, and to forget all about the theory of tragedy being distinct from comedy. We shall see later how and when this theory took shape. For the public of the thirties the essential was dramatic pleasure; the various kinds of pleasure were not considered to be better if separated. This was a later development: 'Les genres mixtes disparaissent vers 1640' (Bray, *Doctrine classique*, p. 305). A letter of Chapelain, written under the impression of the first run of *Le Cid*, does not differentiate between tragic and comic pleasure: 'Depuis quinze jours le public a été diverti du *Cid* et des *deux Sosies* à un point de satisfaction qui ne se peut exprimer.' This is entirely in line with the impatience shown by Corneille himself when his play was submitted to academic censure: 'J'ai fait le Cid pour me divertir, et pour le divertissement des honnêtes gens qui se plaisent à la Comédie.'

It is time to ask what comedy meant for French playgoers in the decades before Molière revolutionized their concepts. As just used, the word had the general sense of a play, or the place where one could see a play. This use persists in the name of the most famous Paris theatre: La Comédie Française. It is not a theatre that specializes in comedy. In particular, comedy was the name given to plays about ordinary people and everyday life. Corneille in his *Discours* on the dramatic poem was clearly assuming an agreed starting-point:

> The difference between comedy and tragedy is that tragedy needs for its subject an action which is at once famous, unusual, fateful, while comedy is satisfied with a light-hearted action in the hands of ordinary people. Tragedy needs heroes and great dangers; comedy needs anxieties and disappointments befalling its main figures. Both kinds have one thing in common, which is that the action must be complete, finished, that is to say that, when all is over, the spectator must know enough of the feelings of the actors to leave the theatre undisturbed and unpuzzled.
>
> (GE, i. 25)

Incidentally, does any other text suggest as clearly as this the central forces in French classicism, of unity and clarity and serenity? The essential for the French playgoer seems to be to watch a dramatic action which is pleasing on its completion, which leaves no loose ends or doubts, and which puts the audience in a mood of intellectual repose.

Perhaps for our understanding one should repeat yet once more that in the 1630s the comic and the tragic modes are not separable and exclusive. The pastoral combined them both, as did the tragicomedy. It would be interesting to know with more exactitude what each mode had to offer. The tragic was not the Renaissance type of noble song; it made more use of the impressive, the grand, and the paradoxical. D'Aubignac, in many ways a more typical theatregoer than Corneille, has some interesting remarks on this. The best actors, he writes in his *Pratique du Théâtre*, should be given parts that keep them a long while on stage. Why? 'Parce que ce sont les meilleurs, qui donnent le plus de satisfaction à ceux qui les entendent . . . parce qu'ils sont les mieux vêtus et partant les plus agréables au peuple . . . parce qu'ils ont les plus belles choses à dire, et les plus grands sentiments à faire éclater, en quoi consiste toute la force et tous les charmes du théatre' (ed. Martino, p. 278). The comic mode relied on laughter, as we have seen from the *Examen* to *Mélite,* either by portrayal of absurd and traditional types, such as *le Capitan* or *le Docteur*, or in a manner which Corneille claimed to have introduced with *Mélite*, which conveyed polite conversation and curiously devised imbroglios. Thus in the comic as in the tragic kind of dramatic pleasure there are signs of what Molière and Racine were to provide and which has come to be called classical. But comedy in the 1630s did not, I think, depend on wit and laughter so much as on relief and relaxation at the spectacle of human folly, or of human failure to reckon with the vagaries of chance. In a sense this was one of the foundations on which Molière could build. He made the comic spectacle into a critique of behaviour and a display of intelligence, which after all is what the seventeenth century understood by wit.

There are signs of this in Corneille's comedies, but still more in the play mentioned in Chapelain's letter as having given a degree of pleasure achieved only by *Le Cid*, that is Rotrou's adaptation of Plautus: *Les Sosies*. The wit displayed in Mercury's bullying of the servant Sosie is in essence Molièresque. Being a god, Mercury can know everything, and this supplies to both Rotrou and Molière the device of persuading a simple man that he has no right to his own name. If this device had not given great pleasure I am sure that it would not loom so large in both comedies. Let us not imagine or expect too much from the Marais audience, noisy, no doubt, as well as intelligent. The pleasure was in fact naïve, that of seeing the natural cowardice of the servant opposed by the mischievous know-later, when the Marais theatre had made large profits out of Rotrou's the reason and conscience of his victim so that (as in Molière) Sosie begins to wonder whether he really is himself:

> Il l'a déjà sur moi par la force emporté
> Et la raison encor semble de son côté. . . .
> Démarche, taille, port, menton, barbe, cheveux,
> Tout enfin est pareil et plus que je ne veux.
> Mais cet étonnement fait-il que je m'ignore?
> Je me sens, je me vois, je suis moi-même encore
> Et j'ai perdu l'esprit si j'en suis en souci.

We are here dealing with classical material, used in a new way. Rotrou treats a mythological theme, stressing the witty effects on all-too-human persons. Molière, taking up the theme thirty years later, when the Marais theatre had made large profits out of Rotrou's comedy and its adaptation *La Naissance d'Hercule* (cf. ed. Mélèse, p. 13), may have been attracted by the chance of a box-office success (which in fact he achieved with a run of thirty performances), but Rotrou has clearly enabled him to make the subject even less mythological and more comic: 'Molière a bien compris ce qu'un tel sujet devait être pour être accepté par les spectateurs: il en a tiré une pièce franchement comique, et fait une satire irrévérencieuse des divinités mythologiques' (ed. cit., p. xviii).

To speak of the new wit of the 1630s is not to forget that the old forms of comic gaiety continued, in the farce, in the chanson, which seems to have been demanded after all performances, in the Tabarin pieces, as we have seen, and in experiments of which an outstanding example is by Pierre Corneille himself. The first performance of *L'Illusion comique* may have preceded Rotrou's comedy by some eighteen months. This has all the love of novelty which we associate with Corneille: the romanesque content of the tragicomedy, a magician, even actual discussion of new forms of theatre, and as a final *coup de théâtre* the discovery that the hero is not dead, because it was all only a play. After line 1745 we have what must be one of the most interesting stage directions in seventeenth-century drama:

On tire un rideau et on voit tous les Comédiens qui partagent leur argent.

So the title in itself is a remarkable piece of wit. The illusion is that of playing, the subject is the art of the actor. In a way, it can be seen as the theatre coming of age, being self-conscious to the point of giving the audience a discussion of what audiences like. It tells us something of the social attraction of the kind of play which appeals to more than one class of person:

> Cessez de vous en plaindre; à présent le theatre
> Est en un point si haut qu'un chacun l'idolatre
> Et ce que votre temps voyait avec mépris
> Est aujourd'hui l'amour de tous les bons esprits,
> L'entretien de Paris, le souhait des Provinces,
> Le divertissement le plus doux de nos Princes,
> Les délices du peuple, et le plaisir des grands.
> . . . C'est là que le Parnasse étale ses merveilles
> Les plus rares esprits lui consacrent leurs veilles. . . .
> Le Théatre est un fief dont les rentes sont bonnes.
>   (1781 ff.)

Before summing up even so casual an account as this of the dramatic production of a decade we must say something of another of Mondory's experiments at the Marais, probably a month or so after *Le Cid*, written by a young man on the staff of Richelieu, Desmarets de Saint-Sorlin. His play *Les Visionnaires* was still praised, Rapin says, in the 1670s, and, like that of Corneille just mentioned, it contains some discussion on plays, with special reference to the new habit of 'strict' writing, of observing the unities of time and place and action, and incidentally reveals the reason of such concentrated writing: everything must be done to avoid distracting the mind of the spectator from what he is actually watching. The evidence is worth adding to that quoted above from Corneille:

> . . . Il faut poser le jour, le lieu qu'on veut choisir
> Ce qui vous interrompt ôte tout le plaisir.
> Tout changement détruit cette agréable idée
> Et le fil délicat dont votre âme est guidée
> Si l'on voit qu'un sujet se passe en plus d'un jour,
> L'auteur, dit-on alors, m'a fait un mauvais tour;
> Il m'a fait sans dormir passer des nuits entières,
> Excusez le pauvre homme, il a trop de matières.
>
> (ed. H. G. Hall, lines 579 ff.)

This comedy is almost without plot; its subject is people, and their notions. Mme de Sévigné said of it: 'nous trouvâmes que c'était la représentation de tout le monde; chacun a ses visions plus ou moins marquées' (*apud* Hall, op. cit., p. lxxxi). If space allowed one could show how like is the content of Desmarets's comedy to a contemporary piece of little value, *L'Hôpital des Fous* of a certain Beys, which possibly goes back to a Renaissance skit known in England, *The Hyeway to the Spittel House*, and to the vogue of Sebastian Brant's *Ship of Fools*. These subterranean connections of literature suggest that the masterpieces which survive are in fact only relics of many individual attempts to say something. We should not think of the masters of literature expressing their grand ideas and neat formulae in a vacuum: they are usually more immersed in the activity of their contemporaries and in the spirit of their age than we who read only their works can ever realize. This is seen in the way we look at a certain restricted production such as we have considered in this chapter. From our distance in the 1970s it is clear the 1630s in Paris produced one or two plays of note. But, if we wish to understand what was actually going on in the world of the Paris theatre of that time, we must remember that these one or two plays are but a few out of many, and that their force depends on the stimuli of many kinds given and received. We are entitled to say, I think, that in this decade French interest in the drama rose to a new pitch, and that the many plays, of many kinds, which interested intelligent audiences included some that in retrospect we can see were the artistic answer to the efforts of a century and more. A form had been found, and entertainment was supplied that in some cases has had a long life. What is more important, the practice of that form was such, in attraction and in wit, that writers were tempted to go still further on the way towards concentration. The next decade will see even more remarkable plays, even more concentrated; an increasing distaste for mixing two kinds of theatre; a success in suggesting one sort of theme, which even a Corneille has not succeeded in achieving before 1640.

4
The Forties

To their first hearers the plays of the 1640s must have seemed very much like those we have been studying from the previous decade. Indeed, a decade is such an artificial division that it might not occur to contemporaries to separate plays by such a barrier. Yet to us, who study a form of classical art, the two groups are very different, so much so that we divide them, for our convenience, into two groups. In both we are presented with similar variety of entertainment, and perhaps also a similar sense of a newly discovered form, which seems to promise developments. Yet the plays of the 1640s have more than this. They have the stamp of achievement, as those of 1635–7 seemed to bear the stamp of attractive novelty. Corneille in particular can no longer be called one of a gifted half-dozen dramatists. He still experiments, but his dramatic pieces are no longer attempts: they are achievements, seen to be such by penetrating contemporaries, and their reputation has been confirmed and increased with the passing of time and the changes of taste. So that we may speak of *Mariane* as a classical work, but of *Cinna* as a classic as well.

In the ten years after 1640 Corneille produced nine plays, and of these at least four are still read and seen with pleasure. This is not so with those of his colleague Rotrou, who also produced nearly a play a year. At the time they must have seemed comparable to those of Corneille. At no time is it easy to see what will satisfy the taste of a later time.

For the three years 1640–2 Lancaster's comprehensive *History* discusses twenty-two tragedies, involving ten authors. In the same three years he finds no less than twenty-five tragicomedies and only eight comedies. If these figures suggest any important conclusion, it is, perhaps, that classical plays are rare. The chief theatrical attraction, then as now, was probably novelty rather than regularity, sensation more than concentration. The baroque attraction of disguise, *trompe-l'œil*, ambiguity, plays within plays, etc., which Jean Rousset has found in dramas of the 1630s, is not a quickly passing phase. If we are studying the new French taste for theatre, all this must be taken into account; from such a point of view one play is as good as another. Accurate information about all the known plays—the sort of material which Lancaster provides—is the only basis for knowing what happened. But few things are more ephemeral than drama. Most plays are soon lost from memory, as they are from view. Once we have noted the facts of quantity and variety of the plays, then we are free to proceed to study of a quite different phenomenon, the durability of certain plays, in contrast to the short life of the majority.

Our problem here is to discern the qualities which, in the opinion of most good judges, make such tragedies as *Horace* and *Polyeucte* inexhaustible. What have such works that allows them to provide continued enjoyment, on the stage and for the modern reader, for the neophyte as for the scholar? Deep questions are raised here, which concern the genius of Corneille, the nature of French classical art, and the relation between the classical viewpoint and the French mind. Let us not rush to solve them, but let us be aware that they exist.

Our first information about *Horace* comes again from Chapelain, who in a letter dated 19 February 1640 writes that Corneille's 'a fait une nouvelle pièce du combat des trois Horaces et des trois Curiaces, où il y a une quantité de belles choses et du même esprit du Cid'. Surely not many judgements, even of greater critics than Chapelain, have stood the test of time better than this. The story of the play, if we mean by that the events and the people who take part, may still be read in Livy. But the playwright seems to show equal desire to use the story as basis, and to get away from its actual details. The choice of the champions, the actual fight, the brother's murder of his sister, none of these are vividly shown on stage; they

are reported, as the return of Thésée is reported in *Phèdre*, or the
orders of Amurat in *Bajazet*. The drama is not eventful in the usual
sense; it consists in oppositions, in suggestions of temperament,
mood, sense of values. M. Adam has described the play as the
picture of a French family in time of war, but even this is no complete description. As I have written elsewhere:

The situation is suggested, the only present reality is the force of opposition
of mood and idea. The situation is admitted extraordinary, even unique,
cruel to the point of causing a mutiny in the two armies: it is only allowed
to develop by special dispensation of the gods. The characters themselves
find no explanation of it. We only know of its development as revealed
in the characters; hearing the tale of the son's valour, the father rejoices
(as he has sworn to kill him on a false report of his cowardice), the sister
hardens to desperate resentment. Horace appears once more, tired, irritable
and boastful; his mood rouses his sister to curses which goad him to the
pitch of striking her down. At his trial he is unrepentant and others have
to settle the dilemma of whether such a man can stay in society or whether
that society can sentence its own deliverer.

(*Horace*, Blackwell edn., p. 7)

Horace is such an exceptional play that we can only be fair to its
originality by having the action in some sort present to us. It might,
if needed, serve by itself to justify French classical tragedy as an art
form. By that I mean that the sort of drama we have watched
emerge in and through the experiments of the Renaissance, and
under the powerful impetus of Richelieu, here seems at a bound
almost to have achieved pure form. Not that the play is perfect, or
that it has kept its full impact up to our own day. But beside it *Le
Cid* seems a sketch, an overture (the actual word I take from
Klemperer, *Pierre Corneille*, 1933, p. 190). Here at last is complete
concentration on a subject that is not historical, though we think
that we are watching the acts of people concerned in the early history of Rome. The real subject is a clash of temperament, of
Weltanschauung, of personal attitude to public duty. A wealth of
rhetoric is devoted to illumine this central conflict, which in itself
is not physical, nor accidental, nor just sensational. We feel it rather
to be essential, something in the nature of modern consciousness;
only rhetoric, unreal language, could suggest such deep conflicts of

the modern spirit. Only the tightest structure could make the central issue felt throughout all the encounters of the play. That issue, as I see it, is the opposition of two attitudes to the state. Both are found in honourable men, men of courage, who risk death for their country. But one of these does so without question:

> Rome a choisi mon bras, je n'examine rien. (488)
> . . . Albe vous a nommé, je ne vous connais plus. (502)

Such a man has no conscience apart from his civic duty, in which, of course, he has great pride. For him that duty has no rivals. Beside it, desires, comforts, pleasures, family ties, simply do not count. He is opposed by one equally brave, for whom these things do count, who admits the claim of the state, but insists on keeping his sense of the greater community of humanity:

> Je rends grâce aux Dieux de n'être pas Romain
> Pour conserver encor quelque chose d'humain. (481-2)

This opposition is central to the play: both the fight and the murder are subordinate to it; they are symbols of it, not events in their own right. The famous imprecations of Camille light up one side of it; the dignified words of the father firmly enforce the other. The trial of the last Act weighs both sides and comes to no conclusion: the man on trial is both murderer and hero. It is hard to imagine a more dramatic theme. Our gaze is kept on the central conflict and is not distracted by external matters, by change of place, by events in temporal sequence. *Horace* is proof that French classical drama produced pleasure from the clash of ideas, not of events or even of individuals. It is, in a sense, Cartesian.

The play presents us with this paradox: it seems to be about events, about people, about history; it is really about a single dilemma, illustrated in the sequence of scenes. The dramatic illusion is that we watch events; the pleasure comes from the fact that the form has liberated us from dealing (as in real life we are always dealing) with events: we are free to look at an issue.

And the issue is still with us. In the problem of the patriot Corneille has discovered a conflict which still divides families. Modern war puts us all in somewhere between the extreme positions that confront each other in this play. Faced by a world war, or a civil war, or by conscription, or the draft, we are faced by something that makes some say: 'My country, right or wrong.' It makes others say: 'Patriotism is not enough.' It makes many others take up a compromise somewhere between these two positions.

In making a play out of this sort of clash the classical dramatist observes two principles, for which Corneille has not, perhaps, been given credit. He presents extremes, so that the dramatic tension can be at its greatest. And he presents both sides fairly, so that we have, not his opinion, but the full dramatic force of two contradictory opinions. *Horace* is an impartial play. It was once taken to be an indictment of militarism, which presented the out-and-out soldier as a sort of brute. Now academic criticism has swung right in the other direction. The soldier is praised for his devotion and his crime is condoned; it is not in fact a crime, since it is the condition of his 'self-mastery'. I cannot think that Corneille indulged in any of these sophistries. I see no words in his text which allow me to say on which side of the question he stood, or which side he commends to his spectator. I agree with M. Vedel that in this play 'il reste aussi invisible derrière son oeuvre que Shakespeare' (*Deux Classiques français*, p. 209). And to escape the one-sided importunity of academic critics we might well listen to the personal impressions of a natural critic. In a travel diary which he called *Retour du Tchad* André Gide wrote a page of which I cannot forbear to quote the main points:

I am re-reading *Horace*, a play I find extremely exasperating, in which all seems forced and obvious, because it is all so abstract. Yet one gets caught out. After a dragging and pompous start, Corneille rises to the heights. The figure of Curiace is beautifully done, and his opposition to Horace just right. This part repays most careful reading. The entire second Act is splendid, Corneille at his best: I know nothing finer of its kind. The farewells of Father Horace to Curiace are most delicate and sensitive. . . . The whole of Act III is poor, and in places very bad. And Camille's monologue in Act IV is absurd . . . what actress could make that come across? Yet Act V is admirable, from every point of view. How satisfying that argument should follow action and thus round off the tragedy.

(p. 162)

Perhaps Corneille never again achieved a dramatic structure as compelling as *Horace*. But the new power, and the classicism, are strikingly in evidence in the years following 1640. The apparent subject of *Cinna* is a Roman conspiracy, forestalled, discovered, mastered. The scruples of the plotters, the heroics of the Emperor, may seem to strike no chord in our twentieth-century outlook, but for those who like Corneille already the play is seen to be a marvel of construction. Let us listen to a recent editor:

The cardinal virtue of the French classical theatre is not simplicity of subject-matter; this had been achieved to perfection by the static and declamatory tragedies of the Renaissance. In the best seventeenth-century works, the crisis enacted is one of action, mainly psychological no doubt, but not consisting merely of suffering and lamentation. One of the greatest contributions of Corneille and his rivals to the development of French tragedy was the invention of *peripéties*, i.e. *coups de théâtre*, sudden changes of situation in the course of a drama. The action of *Cinna* is remarkable for the successive 'shocks' administered to the audience, which is kept in perpetual suspense. . . . There is hardly a weak link in the chain. . . . In *Cinna* Corneille proves that a tragedy composed almost entirely of mental conflicts can be just as theatrical as a drama of blood and violence.

(*Cinna*, ed. Watts (1964), p. 15)

Corneille's own judgement on his play, made at a time when a change in taste provoked him to defend it, showed him to be conscious of the centre of attraction in the new drama, and to be working his way towards a Racinian kind of play, where the simplicity of action is such that the entire dramatic pleasure comes from the suggestive power of the language: 'the subject is easily grasped, neither overweighted with incident nor cluttered up with information of past events; this, no doubt, was one reason for the approval it earned from all sides. The audience enjoys following things as they happen, with no necessity to think back over the past if they are to grasp what is going on.' The change in taste which caused Corneille to write an *Examen* for each of his plays was a small affair compared with what has happened since. Our interest in the plays (to judge from what is said about them to students) is an interest in psychology, and in the degree of tragic emotion generated by the dramatic action. The first audiences were unmindful of both these things. Their taste was for rhetoric, for heroics, for statements of despair, exaltation, vengeance. They were not readers but spectators and, even more, auditors, of an actor or an actress who could utter grand language; in this play they could hear a woman defy an emperor:

> Il peut faire trembler la terre sous ses pas
> Mettre un roi hors du trône, et donner ses Etats,
> De ses proscriptions rougir la terre et l'onde,
> Et changer à son gré l'ordre de tout le monde,
> Mais le coeur d'Emilie est hors de son pouvoir. (940-3)

This rhetoric animates all the plays, and without it the classical play is unthinkable. It allowed Corneille to escape the demon of moralizing which beset poets who cultivated serious drama. It allowed him even to portray a criminal queen in the raging fury of Cléopâtre. He admitted later that *Rodogune* was his own favourite among his plays, and again he revealed his criteria, which (to judge from its enduring success) were also those of his public. This subject of a moral monster, which Lessing in a famous attack thought vicious and immoral, was in the eyes of its creator a beautiful subject: he wrote of his play: 'Varied elements meet in the play, a grand subject, new situations, powerful verse, sound arguments, warmth of passion, love tenderly expressed, friendship, all happily merged so as to create a tension that mounts from Act to Act.' Voltaire declared that even the absurdities in this play were compelling, such was the tyrant's position of power over the lives of others. The queen presents her crimes as progressive revelations of an irresistible need of power:

> Je vous connaissais mal.
>   —Connais-moi tout entière. (503)

> Que tu pénètres mal le fond de mon courage
> Si je verse des pleurs, ce sont des pleurs de rage. (1387-8)

> . . . Va, triomphe en idée avec ta Rodogune
> Au sort des Immortels préfère ta fortune,

Tandis que mieux instruite en l'art de me venger
En de nouveaux malheurs je saurai te plonger. (1395–8)

Such lines make one wonder whether even a tragic poet such as Racine could have imagined Agrippina as he did, had he not had before his eyes this splendid sketch of female fury.

Corneille's mastery of rhetoric is found in all his plays, and was no doubt their chief attraction, but never was his skill more subtle or his imagination more commanding than in his first attempt to make tragedy out of martyrdom, in the play which preceded *Rodogune*. In the eyes of many scholars *Polyeucte* is Corneille's masterpiece. Of it Rigal wrote: 'c'est la perfection enfin obtenue du genre tragique, c'est l'apogée du génie cornélien' (*De Jodelle à Molière*, p. 230). At first sight it would seem to be a counterpart to *Horace*, centred on a religious fanatic as the former play was centred on a military fanatic. Certainly the Christian convert speaks in the same tone as the soldier, of unquestioning obedience to a principle that makes all human obligations secondary and subordinate: 'Je ne vous connais plus si vous n'êtes chrétienne' (1612). Yet perhaps the strength of the play comes from the success with which a grotesque and extraordinary situation is brought close to reality. The conflicts of religion, the choice between God and Caesar, were not unknown within the families who frequented the Marais theatre. As Vedel says: 'For nearly a hundred years France had seen many highly born and worthy Huguenots turn into contempt of official religion, rebel against the state, and sever human ties with the intransigence of a Polyeucte. Many a personage of considerable culture and morality had judged such fanaticism in the same way as Pauline and Severus did' (op. cit., p. 118). The frontispiece of the first edition reinforced this suggestion by a picture of the martyr attired in seventeenth-century costume. Tallemant, indeed, has left a vignette of a Protestant *inspiré* even more extreme than Polyeucte: 'On fut obligé de protéger sa femme qu'il menaçait de sacrifier pour suivre l'exemple de l'antique patriarche et montrer sa soumission aux décrets du Seigneur.' In working over his sources Corneille creates an essential character, and one would have thought that this in itself was a valuable clue to his intention. As he had created Emilie, so he now adds Sévère, the gallant pagan lover, whose role it

c

is to bring out the struggle in Pauline between romantic and married
love. The lines often reach a new pitch of theatrical romanesque:

> O trop aimable objet qui m'avez trop charmé,
> Est-ce là comme on aime, et m'avez-vous aimé? (495–6)
>
> Trop rigoureux effets d'une aimable présence
> Contre qui mon devoir a trop peu de défense. (537–8)
>
> Adieu, trop vertueux objet, et trop charmant.
> — Adieu, trop malheureux et trop parfait amant. (571–2)

Yet the chief struggle of the play is not between lover and husband,
but between husband and wife. This, in a play which depends so
much on rhetoric, is almost a denial of rhetoric. Professor Tanquerey
regarded *Polyeucte* as Corneille's most realistic play: 'Corneille n'a
jamais montré plus clairement combien la vérité est plus noble et
plus puissante que tout ce qui n'est pas fondé sur elle et comme
elle dissipe aisément le romanesque même le plus poétique' (p. 472).
Those who glibly repeat that a martyr who desires to die cannot be
a tragic figure should pay some attention to the way Corneille poses
his problem. His martyr indeed desires death, but even more does he
desire that nothing should come between himself and his God. For
one who regards his commitment as total any earthly tie is an
encumbrance—his own word is obstacle:

> Je consens ou plutôt j'aspire à ma ruine,
> Monde, pour moi tu n'as plus rien.
> Je porte en un coeur tout chrétien
> Une flamme toute divine,
> Et je ne regarde Pauline
> Que comme un obstacle à mon bien. (1139–44)

In a tense scene between husband and wife the two positions are
put. Is not this the finest use of stichomythia in classical French?

> Quittez cette chimère, et m'aimez.
>   — Je vous aime
> Beaucoup moins que mon Dieu, mais bien plus que moi-même.
> — Au nom de cet amour ne m'abandonnez pas.
> — Au nom de cet amour, daignez suivre mes pas.

— C'est peu de me quitter, tu veux donc me séduire?
— C'est peu d'aller au ciel, je vous y veux conduire.
— Imaginations.
                    — Célestes vérités.
— Etrange aveuglement.
                    — Eternelles clartés. (1279–86)

The wrong question to ask about all this is what Corneille thought, where Corneille stood. He stands outside his creation, like Shakespeare and Molière; his objectivity is the condition of his dramatic picture being complete, round, fair, universal. His play may well contain nothing about martyrdom that is not in the New Testament. But it is fair to reality as we know it, and being so, it has power and persuasive force, even when read, rather than seen.

At the risk of seeming to confine our account of a decade to the work of one man, we must say, what is obvious to all students, that Lancaster was right in calling the 1640s 'the period of Corneille'. In the 1630s he was one of a group, but with *Horace* and the tragedies of the next four years he produces plays which 300 and more years later seem, as no doubt they did to many of his contemporaries, incomparable. Certainly his own powers were never to be shown with such mastery. *Nicomède*, at the end of our decade, is an interesting and a classical play. The Fronde seems to have either silenced him or coincided with his silence as regards the theatre. As we shall see, his work in the sixties is that of an experienced craftsman; it continued to give pleasure. It would be a bold statement to say that it still does so.

We pass now to a feature as to which only conjecture is possible. Was it the success of his tragedies that encouraged Corneille to go back to comedy? As we have seen, he spoke of tragedy and comedy as equal forms of entertainment. He even used both modes within a single play. But in the 1640s he seems to have discovered that concentration on the tragic mode left no room for the comic; there is none in the plays we have considered in this chapter. Yet, as far back as 1629, in the Preface to *Mélite*, he had argued that a modern comedy was possible, without gross characters and physical effects. He had made good his claim in a series of comedies which relied on amusing conversation, set in a context of human error. All his comedies are in fact versions of the comedy of errors. It may well have been the actor Jodelet who asked for another play in the style of *Le Place Royale* or *La Veuve* or *L'Illusion comique*. At all events he wrote an adaptation of a play by Alarcón (thinking it was by Lope) and it was played at the Marais, probably in 1643, under the now famous title of *Le Menteur*. Of it he said in his *Épître*: 'I wrote *Le Menteur* in reply to many requests, to satisfy the typical French love of variety. After so many poems wherewith our best writers have enriched the stage, a desire was felt for something lighter, for entertainment.' This was the way he often spoke of comedy, as being *enjoué*, which we might translate as 'light, good-humoured, lively'. He seems to have thought that comedy might be renewed by being made more polite, civilized, witty. This is an idea for which he has not been accorded much credit. It is not at all what classical comedy became in the hands of Molière. Indeed the remarkable thing about Molière's Paris beginnings is that he avoids polite comedy, and returns to farce.

The comic appeal of *Le Menteur* seems to come from a clever mixture of chance, disguise, and deceit, the lying in itself being attractive. It is done partly in self-defence, partly to further a lover's fortunes, and mostly as the play of imagination on reality. Since things do not go his way Dorante spins a web of make-believe which at least attracts attention. As Lancaster neatly remarks: 'What attracted Corneille was the gaiety rather than the morality of the theme. He saw that the hero was not a villain . . . He is nearer to Tartarin than to Tartuffe' (II. ii. 444). When he serenades the wrong lady, he has no way out except to imagine things different from what they are. For after all, to pit ingenuity against fact is a comic design:

> Le ciel fait cette grâce à fort peu de personnes
> Il y faut promptitude, esprit, mémoire, soins,
> Ne se brouiller jamais, et rougir encor moins. (934–6)

Our pleasure is in watching this ingenuity, and its inevitable outcome: the facts catch up with the inventive Dorante: 'Les gens que vous tuez se portent assez bien' (1164). In spirit this is at times near to Molière. Mascarille and Scapin seem to owe some of their verve to Corneille. And the same could be said of the esthetic of the ending. Classical comedy treats endings with considerable *sans-gêne*. The play is over, the illusion is broken, in *L'Illusion comique* by showing the players counting their takings, in *Le Menteur* by arranged marriages. In his *Examen* Corneille admitted that the ending of his Spanish source was somewhat harsh for French taste. A similar objection was made to the way Molière ends *L'École des femmes*: 'In my opinion, this way of ending the play was somewhat harsh and crude; a marriage less forced would have pleased people better. This made me endow him with an inclination for Lucrece in the last Act, so that after the confusion over the assumed names has been cleared up, he can pass things off by making a virtue of necessity and the play may end with everyone satisfied.' Incidentally, one feature of this ending was that the dutiful obedience of the daughters was expressed in two lines already used in the tragic context of *Horace*. There is a certain piquancy in such repetition: it underlines the point that sentiments may be expressed, in much the same terms, in the comic mode as in the tragic. Was it so harsh of Molière to parody Corneille's tragedy when Corneille was ready to parody himself?

Such in rough outline seems to be Corneille's personal contribution to the plays of the 1640s. It is so much more successful and enduring than that of others that one has to redress the balance and say something of the plays which had some success. Of the brilliant writers of the 1630s Mairet contributes little. Tristan wrote at least three tragedies: *La Mort de Sénèque*, which worked over passages of Tacitus, and may have served Racine; *La Mort de Chrispe*, played only, it seems, by Molière's first company (1644); and *Osman*, which Lancaster thinks was probably played first in 1647, and which again is something of a source book (as regards Turkish customs at least) for Racine. Du Ryer followed the success of his *Saül* (1640) with a tragicomedy on *Bérénice* (1645, not the queen of Corneille and Racine), and a tragedy *Scévole*, which might be worth detailed investigation. Lancaster notes that it was not only played by Molière's two companies but at the Hôtel de Bourgogne, and seems to have kept its appeal as long as up to 1721, when the *Mercure* wrote that in it 'les sentiments élevés et la grandeur romaine s'y font sentir à chaque instant.'

More important for our present purpose are the later plays of Rotrou, who died in 1648. His *Bélissaire*, called a tragicomedy though it ends with the death of the hero, seems to have given Racine one of the impressive scenes of *Britannicus*, where the hidden Nero dictates Junia's cold reception of her lover. His play on *Venceslas*, like *Le Cid*, was first called *tragi-comédie* and later changed to 'tragédie'. It is interesting for other resemblances to *Le Cid*. The source was a Spanish comedy by Rojas, which Lancaster calls a 'moving drama of fraternal rivalry and paternal self-sacrifice'. Rotrou removes the comic scenes and offers in prince Ladislas a companion figure to Rodrigue and to the Syroès of Rotrou's last play *Cosroès*. These plays show the difficulties which had to be overcome if the new art form was to give full satisfaction. The character study is at times of great interest, but has to be helped out by the plot. Possibly the reason why Rotrou's plays have not kept their appeal is that the plot and its details interfere with poetic suggestion. To keep the plot nearly out of sight, as Corneille several times did, was a rare achievement. As we should expect, the complexity required to keep up the dramatic interest interferes with the simplicity of structure and concentration. Should we be far wrong in thinking that, for all the plays considered in this chapter, the illusion of an interesting character was demanded both by the public and by the actor, who may well have asked for his part? This would explain the recurrence of certain theatrical characters, such as the good prince (Ladislas, Rodrigue, Syroès, Nicomède) and the virago or stepmother (Cléopâtre, Syra, Arsinoe). In fact, as Professor Knight explained (*The French Mind* (1952), pp. 53–69), the structure and range of characters are strikingly parallel in *Cosroès* and *Nicomède*: both plays have a king, a scheming wife, two princes, one the rightful heir and the other his rival, and two women, one being the second wife, the other in love with the hero. Is not this scheme suggestive? Should we be wrong to suppose that both audiences and actors liked this sort of conflict, the clash of dynastic and personal interests, of duty and nature, of indecision and the intervention? We might add that the real spice of the show lay in the wit that condensed situations of this sort into a challenging formula, as, for example, this: 'Ravissez votre bien qu'on ne vous la ravisse' (*Cosroès*, 242).

Rotrou's remarkable dramatic gifts are seen perhaps to best advantage in *Le Véritable Saint-Genest*, first played in 1645. This excellent play, as we may read it in R. W. Ladborough's pleasant and scholarly edition, must have provided living theatre. An actor promises to act before the Emperor the death of a Christian martyr, and in so doing becomes himself converted. It is thus an entertainment of the same kind as *L'Illusion comique*. In the wake of Lope de Vega's play *Lo Fingido Verdadero* ('Pretence become Truth'), and of a French piece by Desfontaines, the great question of what is true in theatrical illusion is beautifully suggested. One would not say that there is much comic material in the play, but much is said about acting and stagecraft. The text has an ambiguity which perhaps only the actor's voice was competent to resolve. What, for instance, would be suggested to an audience of 1645 by such lines as these?—

> Ce mond périssable et sa gloire frivole
> Est une comédie où j'ignorais mon rôle.
>
> Dieu m'apprend sur-le-champ ce que je vous récite
> Et vous m'entendez mal si dans cette action
> Mon rôle passe encor pour une fiction.

In any case, we have abundant evidence for saying that the new form of the serious play made dramatic enjoyment of high quality possible for the public of the 1640s. The best plays were called tragedies, but I see no real recovery of a deep sense of the tragic. Twice only does Corneille seem to me to have attained real tragedy, and even there the tragic is not his sole preoccupation. Does this lead us to the view that true recovery of the tragic emotion in French classical drama is the work of one man?

After going over the evidence with some care, one may say that we have reached a point at which it may let us down. It suggests that the real achievement of the 1640s was in tragedy. I am not sure. It might well be that the preparation of a new sort of comedy is an even more important development. This cannot be proved; it takes shape in the shadows. But certain facts seem to suggest a trend. We have seen something of the part played by Jodelet in the playing, and perhaps the creation, of *Le Menteur*. The same actor had greater personal share in the work of Paul Scarron, author, wit, celebrity. Scarron adapted Spanish plays and put Jodelet's name in the title, thus *Jodelet, ou le maître-valet* (1643), *Jodelet souffleté* (1646), *Dom Japhet d'Arménie* (1647), *L'Héritier ridicule* (1649). These plays were obviously written not only for but around Jodelet, and his talent for acting farce found a counterpart in Scarron's rough but pointed wit. 'Les comédies de Scarron venaient faire rire autant et plus que la farce' (Rigal, op. cit., 80). This new type of wit became known as 'burlesque', and seems to spring from Scarron's critical sense of the exaggerations of rhetoric. What he did was to parody heroic attitudes, and to fit incongruous language to elegant situations. This was a technique already in the air, in the Spanish picaresque style, in the French farce, and with a gifted actor it produced a new kind of comic valet. Bombast, caricature, parody seem to be the staple elements. We are shown, for example, Jodelet 'seul, en se curant les dents', and saying, no doubt in the tone of heroic comedy,

> Soyez nettes, mes dents,
> L'honneur vous le commande.

We find a rogue saying to a valet disguised as the master that he has already liquidated two in the family:

> Je le ferais encor si j'avais à le faire
> Il ne me reste plus qu'à vous tuer aussi.

It may be that a new force is appearing in dramatic production, a new critical sense, which satisfies what was no doubt an interest in realism. It was much harder to import realism into tragedy than into comedy. Indeed, the conception of comedy as having to do with everyday affairs of ordinary people meant that, sooner or later, authors and actors would exploit its realistic potential. What more effective means of doing so than parody? But Scarron, if unique in his verve and skill, was not alone. Nor was Jodelet. He seems to have had an opposite number at the Hôtel, who acted under the name of Philipin. The Italian actors brought to Paris plays that were not memorized so much as realized. The technique of the *commedia dell'arte* was to act a situation rather than to rehearse a script learnt by heart. This has been described thus:

Italian actors learn nothing by heart. They learn to perform a play by merely looking at the subject for a while before going on stage. . . . A good Italian is a man of parts, who plays by the light of his imagination more than by calling on his memory; a man who suits his acts and words so neatly to those of his partner that he can enter immediately into his role and do what the other requires of him, making us think that they had arranged it so.

(Duchartre, *La Commedia dell'Arte*, 1924)

One of the best of these actors, Scaramouche, seems to have won a disciple in a young bourgeois by the name of Poquelin, who appears in the contract of a new theatrical company that went under the grand title of 'l'Illustre Théâtre'. It was bankrupt within two years, but its leading spirit was to be heard of again, after thirteen years of acting in the provinces.

5
Proto-Critics

NOBODY could study our subject and think that French dramatists of the seventeenth century were careless of criticism. The new drama provoked enormous discussion. Playwrights found fault with each other—like Oscar Wilde's Gwendolen, they found that not only a duty but a pleasure. They explained their own works; they formulated rules of drama and took note of what suited public taste; they discussed why some plays succeeded and others failed. Discussion of drama was not only vigorous; it was organized. The new Academy, and behind it Richelieu, tried to make polemic official, and to spread an orthodox view of disputed matters. Two classical plays caused such a fury of pamphleteering as to merit the name of 'querelle': *Le Cid* in 1637 and *L'École des femmes* in 1662. Since plays could only be published (i.e. made available for any company to play them) some time after they were first performed, it became common practice for the author to defend his play in a preface.

There is something rather impressive about this zeal to impose order and rule. As René Bray puts it: 'La génération de Descartes et de Corneille, de Chapelain et de Balzac . . . organise le Parnasse comme Richelieu le royaume. C'est la génération de l'ordre' (op. cit., p. 358). When one has made allowances for the French love of display, for literary vanity and jealousy, which has been almost a constant in French literary history (one has only to think of the fuss over *Hernani*, or the proscription of works by Baudelaire and Flaubert), it is still remarkable that individual writers accepted and even sought public criticism of their work, that a successful drama-

tist like Pierre Corneille should read a play to a literary circle, that
so much care should be taken to reach an agreed view of drama,
and that theorists should go to the trouble of wide reading, of in-
accessible Latin works, to support their view.

There was nothing either parochial or haphazard about the early
years of French classicism. The fact that France was at war with
Spain did not prevent Spanish plays being adapted for the French
stage. 'J'ai cru que nonobstant la guerre des deux couronnes, il
m'était permis de trafiquer en Espagne' wrote Corneille in presenting *Le Menteur*. If the plots of plays came from Spain the theories
came from Italy. Chapelain wrote to Balzac that if *Le Cid* had been
produced in Italy 'il eût passé pour barbare et il n'y a point
d'académie qui ne l'eût banni des confins de sa jurisdiction', an expression not only of respect for Italian standards but of a desire to
reach an agreed standard. The final court of appeal for these lovers
of order was of course Aristotle. His authority was needed to cover
any innovation. It was reckoned to be one of Corneille's great errors
that he tried to adapt the *Poetics* to his own plays and to get round,
to evade the difficult points.

I was brought up to think of French classical literature as literature written to rule. The rules were specific: verse, the unities,
bienséance, vraisemblance, distinction of *genres*, etc. We were left
to infer that the great dramatists either accepted this control or
evaded it and wrote good plays in spite of it. Like Victor Hugo in
the *Préface de Cromwell*, we speculated on what fine plays Corneille
would have written had people not imposed the rules upon him.
My student history of French literature put the matter in this way:
'The spirit of licence and irregularity displayed by Hardy and his
school could not but displease a public whose ideal now lay in order
and regularity. . . . In 1635 Richelieu was converted. Thanks to his
influence and the advocacy of Chapelain the Rules [sic] finally pre-
vailed, and afterwards came to be looked upon as essential in every
tragedy or comedy worthy of the name.'

Nowadays the literary landscape of seventeenth-century France
looks very different. We see the stage as a battleground between
plays which gave regular stylized pleasure, and plays which gave
sensation, novelty, or thrill (see M. Scherer's view, quoted above,

p. 3). We would be chary of speaking about a 'triumph' of rule, because what we would really be thinking of is a preference on the part of certain dramatists for concentrated and simplified (and hence intensified) drama. From our point of view the work of Racine is the culmination, the triumph, if you will, of such a type. But for contemporaries this was one type among many, not at all triumphant. The interesting thing about it is perhaps the slow start, so to speak, of its appeal, and the growth of a more general sense that here was something of enduring value and of artistic perfection. We need to remember that a spectator as intelligent as Pierre Bayle could bracket the plays on Phèdre by Pradon and Racine as 'deux tragédies fort achevées'.

When we turn to the discussion provoked by plays we are, I fear, bound to be disappointed. The theory of classical drama which we must (albeit painfully) distil from the writings of Chapelain and d'Aubignac, and even Boileau, is cluttered with prejudice and burdened with pedantry. To such critics the important things are not what seem to us now of real importance. The utility of drama, the necessity of this or that character or scene . . . such points offer neither explanation, nor even adequate description, of plays as subtle as *Rodogune* or *Polyeucte*. Far from being a key, what these critics offer is a bar to understanding the phenomena with which they deal. They cannot rightly be called critics: they are proto-critics, paving the way for true criticism by the practice of animated discussion.

We should not expect anything more than this, if we had not all been brought up to think of Boileau as 'le législateur du Parnasse', as judge and arbiter and explainer-in-chief. Criticism as we know it is rare in the seventeenth century. Dryden, Addison, and, as we shall see, Boileau, show gleams of the critical spirit, but they were all defeated, at least in their view of drama, by the twin demons of authority and utility. Only when these had been destroyed by the Enlightenment, by the patient work of Du Bos, Batteux, Voltaire, and Diderot, did it become possible to judge a work by inquiring what it set out to be. Even the great artists had to conform, and to claim that their plays were in line with the *Poetics*, and were conducive to moral improvement. Corneille, indeed, was less conformist in this regard than either Molière or Racine. But it was a specious claim. The esthetic of *Le Cid*, of *Dom Juan*, and of *Bajazet* is not adequately explained by any contemporary. How could it be, in an age when explanation was not even thought necessary? Let us note M. Bray's summing-up of his long enquiry: 'The aim of poetry is the moral instruction of human society . . . the entire esthetic is directed towards this aim and the rules serve only to ensure that the instruction is effective . . . this doctrine leaves no room for the critical sense; the classical poet is emprisoned by his age' (op. cit., pp. 355–7).

Is it not then a waste of time to take seriously a body of discussion so limited and so unhelpful? Not if we know what we are looking for. As a guide to the taste of enlightened theatre-goers, the work of Chapelain and d'Aubignac is indispensable. And the practitioners have always something interesting to say. So has the satirist Boileau, whom recent research has revealed as the very opposite of a dry pedant; a man of flesh and blood, rather, whom Addison visited in 1700, and of whom he wrote: 'He is old and a little deaf but talks incomparably well in his own calling. He heartily hates an ill poet, and throws himself into a passion when he talks of anyone that has not a high respect of Homer and Virgil. I don't know whether there is more of old age or truth in his censures on the French writers, but he wonderfully decries the present and extols very much his former contemporaries, especially his two intimate friends, Arnaud and Racine' (*Works*, ed. Hurd, v. 332).

The central figure in Bray's picture of French classical doctrine is Chapelain: 'For thirty years he skilfully practises the magisterial functions of the critic. He labours, by giving advice and by letter more than by his actual works, to spread respect for classical principles. He is in touch with every writer of any importance, he is in fact their chief propagandist' (op. cit., p. 359).

Chapelain speaks with authority. His critical writings (now easy to study in Hunter's presentation (1936)) consist of the Preface to Marino's *Adone* in 1623, his judgement, in the name of the Academy, on Scudéry's attack on *Le Cid*, his letter to Godeau on the twenty-four hours rule in 1630, his *Discours de la poésie représentative*, and his private correspondence. These all show him as a rather attractive character, well-read, with firm convictions as to the discipline that writers need. We may not like his taste, any more than we need admire his poetry. Boileau and his friends, if we may judge by their satire called 'Chapelain décoiffé', thought him little more than a figure of fun. But he was a man to be reckoned with: we have only to read the lists he drew up for Colbert of French writers who could be relied on for official tributes, and who, incidentally, might be eligible for pensions. These show his very high opinion of Corneille, whom he describes as 'un prodige d'esprit et l'ornement du théâtre français'. He writes as a man called to stem disorder and to curb individualism: 'Nothing is more certain than that pleasure is produced by the observance of order and by what is credible. The Ancients constructed their works on the very principles which people wish now to destroy. If confusion and ineffectiveness in the theatre could give pleasure, it would be for rustics and entirely unable to affect civilized men. I wish to watch a performance and not a jumble' (op. cit., p. 125).

He was clearly a man who disliked distraction; he reproved anything in a play that would take his mind off the main point, or that would weaken the dramatic illusion. And the play was for him something that fascinated as spectacle and as event, never as mere words. His views in this regard should be read as representative of many, perhaps of the sections of the public whom the new school were anxious to please. Listen to him on the pleasure of watching a play: 'The most delicate pleasure is that of being in doubt before a dramatic action which the poet has so contrived that the spectator wonders how it can be resolved. It seems to me a first necessity that no actor should appear or vanish without our knowing why, and a reason being given' (*Opuscules*, ed. Hunter (1936), p. 128). This is not far from the stance of his younger contemporary Dryden, who could write of a play in these terms: 'As in perspective, so in tragedy, there must be a point of sight in which all the lines terminate. Otherwise the eye wanders, and the work is false' (*Essays*, ed. Ker, i. 208).

As to how far Chapelain's writ ran, it is hard to say. Having the support of Richelieu must have given his views an authority which a later generation did not own. It was clearly by pleasing the master that playwrights of the 1630s were likely to prosper. But we should remember that Chapelain was not afraid at times to resist the general trend: he agreed with Godeau that to have all plays in verse was absurd and that rhyme was a tyranny. Why? Because it broke the illusion of actual speech: 'En cela notre langue se peut dire plus malheureuse qu'aucune autre, étant obligée, outre le vers, à la tyrannie de la rime, laquelle ôte toute la vraisemblance au théâtre et toute la créance à ceux qui y portent quelque étincelle de jugement' (ed. cit., p. 126).

Chapelain worked behind the scenes, counselling authors and keeping in touch with the authorities. He wrote no treatise, as did François Hédelin, abbé d'Aubignac. *La Pratique du théâtre*, which seems to have had three editions (1659, 1669, 1715), is a ponderous and careful work, not at all what one would expect from its author, who was said to be impulsive and irascible ('il est tout de soufre' wrote Tallemant). He makes a serious attempt to consider the new drama in the light of Aristotle, the Greek poets, and modern Italian theory. His reading must have been immense. His modern editor counts sixty quotations from Aristotle and no less than 150 examples from ancient drama alone. He professed great admiration for Corneille, but when he had come into public argument with him he erased, in a copy which has luckily been preserved, all favourable references. His printer never made use of his revised manuscript.

His work expresses, often in a blunt way, his own opinions. How far were they shared, and who read him? I cannot answer these questions. As the author of the only comprehensive work of dramatic theory which has survived from its time to ours, he has naturally appeared to be a more important figure than he seems to have been in the discussions of the 1640s and the 1650s. To call him 'le porte-parole de son siècle' is possibly to go well beyond the evidence. I think he was read by Racine; he was certainly refuted by Corneille, but was he taken seriously, and by whom? His importance for us is as a witness rather than as a teacher. In him we have the opinions of an interested observer. He was not a great mind, nor a successful playwright (as Corneille tartly reminded him). He lacks imagination. He has no clear grasp of what we understand by great comedy, or great tragedy, but for all that he is a spokesman for serious drama.

At times d'Aubignac writes like a rationalist: he holds that the authority of Aristotle and the authority of reason are not two authorities but one. Yet his main principle is appeal to the senses. He holds as strongly as Chapelain does that *vraisemblance* is the great principle, since without it the audience cannot have complete illusion. The illusion is not complete if the scene changes, as it would not be complete if the same actor played two parts, as it is not complete when an actor calls for silence: 'It only muddles the spectator's mind if he is asked to imagine two men in one, who think and say contrary and unlikely things. We allow that an actor should break into his speech to call for silence, because we know where we are, and that it is then Bellerose or Mondory speaking and not a god or a king' (op. cit., p. 49). A man who thought in this way would be uneasy with such a play as *Le Véritable Saint-Genest*, but it is not fair to dismiss him as a pedant. He says indeed that all the rules of a dramatic poem are designed to achieve complete illusion: 'elles n'enseignent rien autre chose qu'à rendre toutes les parties d'une action vraisemblables, en les portant sur la scène, pour en faire une image entière et reconnaissable' (op. cit., p. 78).

D'Aubignac is at one with Chapelain in stressing that the chief enemy of illusion is confusion. He wants to be clear what is happening and who is speaking: 'Quand un Roi parle sur la scène il faut qu'il parle en Roi.' He wants the action made easy to grasp, with the minimum of preparation and the maximum of surprise: 'The poet should not fear to spoil his work by overconcentration of events in a short space of time, for, on the contrary, he will only make it the more attractive and wonderful if he can introduce surprising events and extreme passions, and if he consider [the last plays of Corneille], I am sure that he will agree with what I say' (op. cit., p. 124). This seems to me to be good dramatic criticism, none the worse because a quarrel made the critic erase the praise of Corneille. Though the writer might have appreciated Racinian concentration, he shows no sign of being aware of a poetic subject or of the power of tragedy. For him a tragedy is a play about the great; it may end ill or well. Comedy is for him rough drama. All this comes out when he argues that the new term 'tragicomedy' is unnecessary: 'I do not say that we should ban this word, but I think it serves no purpose, since the word tragedy covers poems with happy endings, provided they happen to the great. Furthermore, we do not give to the word tragicomedy its real meaning, since we use it for plays that have no comedy about them, but where all is serious and extraordinary and nothing common or ridiculous' (op. cit., p. 148).

On the other hand this assiduous spectator is aware of the power of words. No one else, to my knowledge, puts the point that the new drama is an affair of words, in which the words are acts: 'the speeches should be like the actions of the persons on stage . . . the entire tragedy consists of speeches; that is the work of the poet and the chief exercise of his mental powers . . . all his invention consists in eloquence' (op. cit., p. 283). This admirable sense of rhetoric can even deliver him at times from the tyranny of moral improvement. Near the end of his work he deals with the objection that a polished speech in verse cannot give any idea of the disorder of passion. It is a sign of critical ability to be aware of the point, and still more to hint the answer, that art may recover the vision of the unity of nature:

. . . writing a speech of pathos as it should be, the great figures of eloquence should be so mixed and merged as to allow the variety of words to convey an image of the restlessness of an anxious mind, worked upon by uncertainty and wracked by extreme feelings. Thus by the order in which things are said one may recompose and fill out the defects of nature's impulses, and allow the effect of the varied figures of speech to transmit some shadow of the disorder of nature.

(op. cit., p. 345)

It is somewhat difficult to seize from these quotations, as it is from the *Pratique* itself, the true figure of d'Aubignac as a critic. The quotations given here illustrate what seem to be valid points in his account of the Paris stage; they do not convey the air of doctrinaire pedantry that hangs over his book. One feels that he had never written a good play, that he is judging from outside, and that he is forced to pontificate and to bolster his prejudice with his learning. This may explain the bitterness of his quarrel with Corneille. Is one justified in reading between the lines of the first *Discourse* on the

dramatic poem and discerning the practical playwright's answer to
La Pratique du théâtre?

> Je hasarderai quelque chose sur cinquante ans de travail pour la scène,
> et en dirai mes pensées tout simplement, sans esprit de contestation qui
> m'engage à les soutenir, et sans prétendre que personne renonce à ma
> faveur à celles qu'il en aura conçues.
>
> (P. CORNEILLE, *Writings on the Theatre*, ed. Barnwell (1965), p. 3)

If this was meant to be an olive branch it was refused, no doubt
because Corneille had studiously avoided all mention of *La Pratique*.
Whatever the relations between the two men it is clear that
Corneille had no sympathy for the 'utility' theory, basic for both
Chapelain and d'Aubignac, which held (*Pratique*, p. 9) that 'la
principale règle du poème dramatique est que les vertus y soient
toujours récompensées'. The first *Discourse* (which stood, let us remember, at the head of the first volume of his collected works in
1660) says almost the converse of this: 'la poésie dramatique a pour
but le seul plaisir des spectateurs.' The whole discussion he regards
as pointless: 'Even this discussion would serve no purpose, since
one cannot please within the Rules and fail to convey some profit at
the same time. Even though utility appears in the guise of attraction,
it is none the less an essential element, and we should do better to
see how it may thus enter rather than to discuss a profitless question
concerning how useful are such poems' (ed. cit., pp. 3–4). So far,
Corneille might be thought to be arguing with d'Aubignac, but he
surely approaches the Racinian esthetic when, after mentioning the
sentences and moral truths which have a place in drama, he comes
on to the second 'utility', which is nothing less than 'la naïve
peinture des vices et des vertus, qui ne manque jamais à faire son
effet, quand elle est bien achevée'. It is this basic conviction which
leads him in the second *Discourse* to attack the Aristotelian concept
of the catharsis, and to dismiss it as 'une belle idée qui n'ait jamais
son effet dans la vérité'. Not only so, but he raises the question
whether there may not be types of tragedy which Aristotle knew
nothing of.

On all these points one feels the dramatist and not the critic is
speaking, that the argument is directed to defending the type of

play he can write and which has proved successful. This may not be criticism in any proper sense, but nobody has better defended the Cornelian play than Corneille himself, and nowhere has he done it better, perhaps, than in his defence of the great dramatic subject:

> It is not that a tragedy on a likely subject is impossible, . . . but that the great subjects, meaning those that stir the power of our passions and oppose their onslaught to the laws of duty or the ties of blood, these must always be extraordinary, and would, indeed, not be believed by the public, were they not enforced either by the authority of history, which it is hard to disbelieve, or by the anxieties of our common lot, which finds the public ready to accept them. It is not likely that Medea should kill her children, Clytemnestra her husband, Orestes his mother, but history tells us that they did so, and when these illustrious crimes are performed before us we all believe they happened.
>
> (P. CORNEILLE, op. cit., cf. p. 70)

One would like to have Racine's gloss on such a passage, for it describes a kind of play from which he departed, but which he no doubt respected, and the form of which was the condition of his art. Literary history has made much of the rivalry between the two men, but we do not have all the relevant facts, and there is another side to the picture. By devoting such art and skill to the presentation in verse of dramatic subjects that would stir the passions of the audience, Corneille perfected a dramatic form which in his *Discours* he never troubled to explain, but which was of priceless value to his successor.

It is now thirty years since René Bray undertook to investigate the formation of classical doctrine in France, and came to the conclusion that Boileau did not invent it but found it ready to his hand in the work of Chapelain and d'Aubignac. In his book M. Bray did much to destroy the notion of Boileau's having been the mentor of the classical artists, and made it difficult even to accept Lanson's dictum that the *Art poétique* is a complete compendium of the classical code. The research on Boileau which has been stimulated by Bray's work has gone much further along the same line. When stripped of legend and submitted to cold analysis it is difficult to see in the famous third *Chant* of the *Art poétique* any but the most banal and obvious counsels to those who would write tragedies and comedies:

> Inventez des ressorts qui puissent m'attacher
>
> Jamais au spectateur n'offrez rien d'incroyable
>
> Des héros de roman fuyez les petitesses
> Toutefois aux grands cœurs donnez quelques faiblesses
>
> Que la nature donc soit votre étude unique
> Auteurs qui prétendez aux honneurs du comique
>
> Etudiez la cour et connaissez la ville
>
> Jamais de la nature il ne faut s'écarter

Fortunately we need no longer be embarrassed by having to call these banalities great principles of art. It is now established that the *Art poétique* was written for the salons, as an entertainment, by a well-known satirist. Mme de Sévigné's letters make this quite clear. 'Je dînai hier avec M. le Duc, M. de La Rochefoucauld, Mme de Thianges, Mme de La Fayette . . . chez Gourville. On écouta la Poétique de Despréaux qui est un chef-d'oeuvre' (15 Dec. 1673. See also letters of 9 Mar. 1672 and 12 Jan. 1674). When she called it a masterpiece, Mme de Sévigné was thinking of the wit and the satire, of the 'air d'honnête homme' which her cousin Bussy Rabutin found in all Boileau's work, and not of theory or literary criticism in our sense. Recent work done by a philologist has shown how full of wit, both in the seventeenth-century sense and in that of today, Boileau's writing can be. It is full of quips, puns, neat allusions, and whimsicality. It is a strange fate that has overtaken so civilized a man, to be held up to posterity as a pedant, a schoolmaster, one who thought poetry was made with reason. Pope knew better, and Keats should have done so. Boileau may not be a great writer. M. Adam thinks his merit has been exaggerated: 'ne pas confondre Boileau avec les grands auteurs de son temps' (*Histoire*, iii. 156). But he was a very polished writer, and even in his old age good company, as we have seen Addison discovered (cf. p. 65 above).*

* Any who still think that the *Art poétique* represents Boileau's entire view of poetry should work through his translation of Longinus, on which he spent much time, and for which he wrote more than one preface (see J. Brody, *Boileau and Longinus* (1958)).

We must place Boileau in a new context if we are to get anywhere near what actually happened, and if we are to see his real relationship to the classics of his day. This is shown more directly in his second Satire, addressed to Molière, and in his Epistle to Racine. His admiration for both artists is undoubted, and we may assume that *L'Art poétique* reflects this, in its stress on accurate psychology, on beauty of dramatic style, on nature and *vraisemblance*. Whether this implied a distaste for Corneille is not so clear, and the Preface to his translation of Longinus on the Sublime, which was published along with *L'Art poétique* in 1674, contains a passage which perhaps comes nearest of contemporary judgements to what we might call good criticism. After quoting from Genesis to illustrate sublime expression Boileau continues thus:

It seemed to me perhaps no bad thing, if I were to convey what Longinus means with this word *sublime*, if I could add to the Biblical passage I have quoted one from another source. Here is one which happily came to mind. It is taken from the *Horace* of M. Corneille. In that tragedy, of which the first three Acts are to my mind the finest writing this great man has given us, a woman who had watched the fight of the three brothers, but who had left before the end, comes to give news to their father that two of the brothers are killed, and that the third brother, seeing no means of further resistance, has run away. Whereupon the old Roman, filled with patriotic fervour, wastes no time over the loss of his two sons and their glorious death, but laments the shameful end of the survivor, who, he says, by his cowardly act has brought eternal shame on the family name. Their sister standing by says: What would you have him do, facing three at once? His laconic reply is: He should have died. Little words, but who does not feel the heroic grandeur they contain? The expression *Qu'il mourut* is all the more sublime for being simple and natural; they allow a glimpse into the very heart of the valiant old man and into a truly Roman temper.

(ed. Boudhors, pp. 47–8)

Surely this is more perceptive criticism than the advice given in the *Art poétique*. Boileau was not in fact the teacher and mentor of the French classical poets, but their disciple. His merit as a critic depends on the vigour with which he showed up the second-rate, and on the respect he had for La Fontaine (his first work was an appreciation of *Le Joconde*), Corneille, Molière, and Racine. But as a dramatic critic in any proper sense Boileau is non-existent.

For the only cogent dramatic criticism of the century (in France at least) we must go to the dramatists themselves. It is not often realized that we have at our disposal Molière's own theory of comedy. The second part of the *Lettre sur 'L'Imposteur'* cannot, in view of the circumstances in which it appeared (cf. René Robert, in *Revue des Sciences Humaines* (1956), pp. 19–53), be other than inspired, possibly dictated, by the master himself. It is a theory which admits the utility of comedy, as we should expect from an author whose play is banned, but which goes on to point out as the central question the nature of what is meant by comic: 'comme il n'est point de genre d'écrire plus difficile . . . il aurait encore besoin de cinq ou six mois pour mettre ce seul discours du ridicule, non pas dans l'état de perfection dont la matière est capable, mais seulement dans celui qu'il est capable de lui donner' ('Grands Écrivains', p. 530).

Briefly expressed, Molière suggests as a theory of comedy the discernment by the mind of those things which nature has made to appear contrary to reason. The comic is for him a shape: 'le ridicule est donc la forme extérieure et sensible que la providence de la nature a attachée à tout ce qui est déraisonnable.' To see this shape of the unreasonable in nature we need above all the clear sight of reason: 'to know what comic means here we must know the reasonable attitude of which it is the opposite, and see exactly what that is. Really to be reasonable is to do those things which one is fitted to do; the outward sign of such reason is *bienséance*, which comes to much the same as the famous *quod decet* of the Ancients.' The *Lettre* goes on to explain that this suitability, from which the comic is a lapse, is to be understood not as a social norm but as something which is in line with the nature and character of a person:

. . . that which is entirely fitting is always based on some standard of good behaviour, just as the unpleasant is based on something grossly out of keeping, and the comic on a failure of reason. Now, if unbecoming conduct is the heart of the comic, it is easy to see why Panulphe's love-making appears comic . . . for the bad effect on others makes him appear so obviously and plainly comic that the dullest spectator can take the point.

This is so, I would hold, because we rate as comic that which is totally devoid of reason.

Several points of importance emerge here. It gives us Molière's view that he had intended nobody to miss the comic side of Tartuffe, and secondly, that this aspect depends on his love, his *galanterie*. He is not therefore comic in his hypocrisy, save that he cannot keep it up, and that he shows this fact in his love-making. If critics and scholars had read this passage with attention, could they have gone so wide of the mark as to think of Tartuffe as satiric and not comic? The mistake we make is to oppose serious and comic. Molière does not suggest this. If for him 'comic' is what is not in keeping with the nature of a person, then all sorts of serious traits of character may be thought of as comic.

Surely we have here one of the chief insights of French classical criticism, put forward not by a critic but by the chief dramatic genius of the age. If so, his view has been strangely disregarded. What is his view? Surely that the domain of the comic goes far beyond what we consider as funny, or what causes us to laugh.* The most disastrous human errors may be envisaged by the mind as comic. As long as we continue to oppose comic and serious, we shall think that anything with tragic consequences cannot be comic. We seem to go by size. We consider lies and deceptions to be matter of tragedy when they are great enough to involve suffering, and to be matter of comedy only when they are small and not, as we say, 'serious'. Molière's language in the *Lettre* knows nothing of any such distinction. It suggests that the difference between tragic and comic does not lie in the gravity of the case, but in the angle of perception. Hitler's talk of peace while he prepared for war was a desperately serious thing: it meant death for millions. But to talk of peace while you prepare for war is comic in the sense of the *Lettre*. To see the mote in your brother's eye and to miss the beam in your own is not funny. It is in Molière's sense comic, and is certainly serious as well. This shows that Molière is working on an

---

* This is my objection to explanations of comedy by the use of Bergson's excellent book. He was analysing laughter, something very different from comedy as a literary form.

opposition quite different from our usual distinction of comic and serious. As he states (see above), the comic is properly opposed to the reasonable. The comic is the absurd, the obviously unreasonable. This is what we find in Molière's own plays. Some of the comic cases which he has imagined are amusing, some are not. The figure of Tartuffe, the *raison d'être* of the *Lettre*, is rarely amusing. Harpagon may amuse us when he asks for 'the other hands', but it is much more than amusing to imagine a man on the limits of humanity: 'Le seigneur Harpagon est de tous les humains l'humain le moins humain.' An actor might make me laugh as he said this, but the suggestion itself is deep and poetic and serious. So serious that Harpagon at one point avows lunacy: 'Mon esprit est troublé et j'ignore où je suis qui je suis et ce que je fais.' Freud would have been fascinated with this imagination of a man so fanatically absorbed in the search for his robber that he grasps his own hand.

I find no comparable statement by a tragic writer which one could put alongside the *Lettre sur 'L'Imposteur'* as defining a classical view of the tragic. Corneille only defined his art after his productive period was over, and under pressure from pedantic attack. Racine never did so at length. All we have are his notes on the Greek dramatists and his answers to critics. Professor Vinaver's comment on the former (*Principes de la tragédie*, p. 49) shows how close to the conceptions of Molière was Racine's basic premiss:

Let the men of theory say what they will, we are not here dealing with any ordinary punishment or gross injustice. Great misfortunes come from the character of those we see in action and from their most deepset impulses, from which they can never escape. It will be through their fault, through a purely human fate, that is to say, that in Racine's plays they will bring about the evil which overwhelms them, and which we find more true and more predictable than any wrath from heaven.

Again we meet the constant preoccupation with nature, with what is basically human, that gives to an artificial form of drama its human centre. Racine never, so far as I know, defined this, but it is implied in his marginal note on Aristotle's comparison of poetry and history:

Poetry is something more philosophical and more entire than history. Poetry deals with the general and history looks only at details. The general is for me whatever a man does that fits in with likelihood and his actual circumstances.

(Vinaver, op. cit., p. 16)

The prefaces to the plays assume these two basic requirements of tragic drama. Like Molière, Racine believed that 'il faut peindre d'après nature. On veut que ces portraits ressemblent.' In the first Preface to *Britannicus* he flashes out against his critics that he knows what they really want:

> What would one have to do to satisfy judges so demanding? The answer would be easy if we did not need to keep to common sense. We could leave the description of things as they are in nature and escape into fantasy. Instead of making the plot straightforward, burdened with few incidents, the kind of action that may happen within one day, and which, moving gradually towards its completion, is maintained only by the interests, the feelings, and the passions of the actors, we could fill it with many matters, things which could not happen within a short space of time, with stage gimmicks, dazzling because they would be unlikely, a mass of speeches in which actors were made to say the contrary of what they would naturally say.

Racine here describes the kind of play popular with his public, and (with the insight of a man baulked of success, perhaps) outlines his own dramatic preference. We may infer, surely, that he was not keen on a play full of action. He asks for only so much action as shall be *soutenu*, or upheld, or made meaningful by the passions of the participants. Again he is in line with what we have discerned as the central tendency of classical drama, the tendency to describe nature rather than to evoke events: not what happens, but what is revealed by what happens. The revelation is also in line with that of Molière's comedy. We watch human nature in conflict with itself, harnessing the will to courses of action which result in ruin. Part of our dramatic pleasure is that we see the whole spectacle, hidden from the actors. M. Picard has thus defined tragic action in Racine: 'L'action tragique est cette action catastrophique que le personnage poursuit parce qu'il le croit efficace, mais que le spectateur sait illusoire ou ironiquement et désastreusement efficace.'

If this is the real discovery made by classical dramatists in the seventeenth century, it is surprising to find no critic even referring to it. As Henri Brémond wrote: 'quand on fréquente les théoriciens littéraires du xviie siècle, on reste confondu de les trouver si peu curieux' (*apud* Vinaver, op. cit., p. 8). This may be because, as La Bruyère suggested, they concentrated on regularity of structure rather than on force of imagination. He comments that there is all the difference between a fine work and a regular work, and takes an example of the former *Le Cid*: 'Quelle prodigieuse distance entre un bel ouvrage et un ouvrage parfait ou régulier.' These notes show that La Bruyère had it in him to be a fine critic. He comments on qualities in Molière which other contemporaries rarely notice: 'quel feu, quelle naiveté, quelle source de la bonne plaisanterie, quelle imitation des mœurs, quelles images, et quel fléau du ridicule'; and his notes on the effect of tragedy stress (as no others do, then or since), the breathless concentration 'qui serre le cœur . . . vous laisse à peine la liberté de respirer. . . .'

It would seem from this admittedly sketchy survey that the practitioners of drama have interesting things to say about it. The theorists on the whole do not. Yet textbooks seem to pay greater attention to anyone who calls himself a critic than they do to the poets themselves. This may account for what I think could be shown to be an error in our perspective (Dryden's word again) of French classical drama. Were the famous Rules either as binding or as important as Lancaster would have us believe? I suggest that they were not.

But this need not surprise us. The Enlightenment liberated the critical sense of Europe, in the sphere of writing as in so many others. As long as it was thought that a play must be both edifying and in line with the precepts of Aristotle, independent criticism was impossible. Critics were shackled: they had to talk about secondary matters; they were not free to discuss the mechanics of dramatic effects. It is ironical that Bossuet, in his effort to convince his age of the immorality of all theatre, should supply a far more satisfying account of the effect of acting than did the book on *La Pratique du théâtre*. Proto-critics, not critics. This they were condemned to be. At this distance of time we can only admire the talent that the French put into a sophisticated (and potentially controversial) form of dramatic art, in which they produced masterpieces they were unable to explain.

6
The Sixties

To any whose interest in the seventeenth century has gone stale, one may recommend a short course in study of the Fronde. This civil war, which some know only from the pages of Dumas, was not the romanesque affair of popular history books: some of its events were terrible and its effects far-reaching. Coming almost at the same time as the Civil War in England, it divides the century. In both countries it might easily have gone the other way, the Royalist way in England, the Parliamentary way in France. But, as if an abyss had been glimpsed, it left behind a new spirit. Gone were the heroics of the 1640s. The tone is more moderate, worldly-wise, cynical, realist. This had some interesting effects in the theatre. We have seen the vogue of the new mock-heroic burlesque. It is no accident that Molière parodies a Cornelian general by putting his words into the mouth of a grotesque character. The rise of a new comedy, one might say, was helped by a cynical spirit, such as affects Restoration drama in England.

A complete history would analyse the dramatic productions of the 1650s as we have done those of the two preceding decades. But this would not greatly alter the picture we already have of conventional stylized drama. Whether or not it was because social conditions were upset in the early 1650s, Corneille wrote nothing between 1651 and 1659. Yet in 1656 was produced the play which, judged by number of performances, proved the greatest French success of the century. *Timocrate* by Thomas Corneille, the younger brother of Pierre, was played eighty times in two Paris theatres. It was, as

Professor Yarrow has shown (in *Orpheus* (1955), pp. 171–82), a play about politics, aristocratic manners, *générosité* and *galanterie*; a play full of striking attitudes, and clever speeches, of disguise and peripety: such ingredients would seem bound to satisfy the Parisian love of the theatre, which was, after all, the driving force behind the entire movement we are here studying. A classical play? Mr Yarrow's answer is interesting:

We are accustomed to thinking of the Seventeenth Century as an age of classicism; and classicism, we are told, is interested in the general and the universal, which it achieves by means of the twin principles of bienseance and vraisemblance. To this view of the Seventeenth Century *Timocrate* is a useful corrective. It is of course a classical play; it obeys the rule of the unities, the stage is never left empty; the bienseances are observed and no action takes place on the stage. On the other hand one can hardly claim that Thomas Corneille was trying to analyse the basic, timeless passions of humanity . . . nor can one seriously call his play vraisemblable. . . . *Timocrate* illustrates perfectly the tension between baroque and classicism which is such an important factor in the literature of the century. *Timocrate* is a baroque subject treated classically. The technique is classical . . . The theme on the other hand, the confusion of identities, is essentially baroque. *Timocrate* is *Amphitryon* or *The Comedy of Errors* in reverse: instead of two men with one appearance we have one man with two appearances. The basic situation is paralleled by the constant use of double-entendre throughout the play—one set of words with two meanings. And underlying the tragedy is the sense that the world is an illusion, that reality is elusive.

The success of such a play is a valuable pointer. *Timocrate* seems to sum up those qualities of surprise and joy in rhetoric which attracted people to the theatre. Is uses with great skill some of the chief attractions of the classical form. To an affected society it supplies affectation in abundance. This audience-appeal—if one may so refer to it—was essential for the life of the drama. It is found in the plays of Thomas Corneille, of Quinault, of Boisrobert, all of which have been carefully studied by Lancaster. We do not neglect them here because we are looking for 'better' plays: no better plays for that stage and that public were perhaps possible. They fulfilled the 'entertainment potential' of a certain dramatic form. What we are looking for in this book is, in fact, something different: plays which both used the form to its maximum and transcended it, in the sense that they supplied enjoyment that lasted, that used the poetic potential of the form so well that spectators, and even readers, of a later age could find in them more than passing enjoyment. It is because various factors seemed to combine, in the years of the new regime, to develop new types of the classical play, that we here consider the plays of the 1660s.

The new trend is seen in two or three convergent features, apparently, but not I think really, unconnected. One of them, which we shall consider in a moment, is Molière's return from the provinces. Another is the magnificence of Foucquet as patron of the arts. Yet another is the personal interest of the young King Louis XIV in the related arts of music, dance, and stage.

It is hard to imagine what dramatists would have done in the seventeenth century without patronage. Molière's prefaces leave no doubt that he considered himself first and foremost a servant of the King, as keen to supply the Court with plays as his father had been to supply furnishings. Perhaps Mazarin, and even more so Foucquet, deserve some of the praise that has been given to Richelieu for encouraging the stage. In the years after the Fronde the chief purveyors of elegant drama, Corneille the younger and Quinault, seem to have written their plays for Foucquet. Quinault, indeed, became so popular that we hear of an authors' cabal against him, which we are told incited him to even greater efforts. His tragedy on *La Mort de Cyrus* transferred to the stage the subtleties of Mlle de Scudéry's novel. Thomas Corneille's *Bérénice* came from the same source, and his *Timocrate* from La Calprenède. It would be interesting to know why it was that the silence of the elder brother coincided with the successes of the younger, who even tried Roman tragedy: *La Mort de Commode* (1657) and played in the presence of royalty, both at the Marais and in the Louvre.

It was again Foucquet who succeeded in tempting Pierre back to the theatre, offering him a choice of three subjects. As we know, he left two of them to his brother, Camma and Stilicon, and chose Oedipus; *Œdipe* was played on 24 January 1659. A dramatic return indeed. The success of the play is understandable. It had the best actors: la Beauchateau, Villiers, Floridor. The author made certain in fulsome verse that the public should know the play was written by request. And then the subject. Racine was later to call it, in his first tragedy, 'le sujet le plus tragique de l'antiquité'. The treatment was to be modern. Corneille explained that he had thought the final scenes of Sophocles too crude for French ears and eyes:

> It was clear to me that what in distant ages had seemed an effect of miracle could to our own cause only revulsion, and that such an unusual and eloquent piece as that describing how the unfortunate prince puts out his eyes, which fills the fifth Act, would offend the delicacy of the ladies whose disapproval would provoke the rest to criticism. As a last point, a love intrigue being absent the play lacks what would give it greatest favour with the public. So I have tried to omit what is unpleasant and have added a love episode between Theseus and Dirce.
>
> (P. CORNEILLE, *Writings on the Theatre*, ed. Barnwell (1965), p. 155)

This passage brings us as near as any document of the time to the esthetic of the first audiences of Racine. It seems incredible that less than ten years before *Andromaque* a play should succeed by avoiding the tragic and by replacing it with heroics and *galanterie*. Yet this was probably the cause of the success of a whole group of plays of the early 1660s: the *Démétrius* and the *Tigrane* of Boyer, the first of which was carefully read by Racine, Gilbert's study of Nero (*La Mort d'Arie et de Patus* (1659)), the pastoral of Quinault (*Les Amours de Lysis et d'Hespérie*), the *Camma* of Thomas Corneille, which in September–January 1661 provoked the greatest crush ever seen at the Hôtel, so that even the 'porteurs de chaises' complained; while at the Palais Royal a week later Molière's acting of *Dom Garcie de Navarre* could not fill the house. It is here that our taste is most sharply at variance with that of the French seventeenth-century public. We think that, in treating Œdipe as he did, Corneille ruined a great tragic subject. We forget that what he made of it was much more in tune with public taste than was *Andromaque*, which immediately called forth a parody. We need this corrective to our preference if we are to realize the paradox of French classicism: the most representative movement in French art was not an immediate success, it took time for its masterpieces to be appreciated by more than a discerning few. Even Mme de Sévigné called it 'good taste' to decry Racine as inferior to Corneille.

We get some idea of the slow disengagement of the durable from the ephemeral if we compare two great successes of 1659, *Œdipe* and *Les Précieuses ridicules*. It was thought that Corneille had surpassed himself and had never shown more dramatic skill ('art') than he did in adapting the harsh and cruel ancient theme. Molière's play was full of deflation, ridicule, of constant preference for nature over art. Yet both were greatly enjoyed, by many people. We can now see that here two traditions met, both of great force, both destined to feed the French theatre for a long time to come. One is the acting of eloquent bombast, the elegant rhetoric; the other is the invasion of the natural into formal art, a naturalism which would make use of realism to enforce fantasy, and which would please with language that was not grand and inflated, but ironical and deflated. When Molière returned to Paris in 1658, after thirteen years in the provinces, he had to please audiences which demanded both bombast and *naïveté*. As an actor of tragedy he won no praise. We cannot tell whether this was due to jealousy, or to his lack of what was considered essential to tragedy, declamation of the required singsong variety. In the delightful play about his own greenroom he teaches an actor to 'recite':

Le comédien aurait récité par exemple quelques vers du roi, de *Nicomède*: 'Te le dirai-je, Araspe . . .' le plus naturellement qu'il lui aurait été possible. Et le poète: Comment, vous appelez cela reciter? C'est se railler; il faut dire les choses avec emphase. Ecoutez moi . . .

and Molière, who is playing this part, goes on to parody the chief actors of the principal tragic theatre, the Hôtel de Bourgogne. Behind these amusing lines lies no doubt personal antagonism as well as theatrical practice, but they show what Molière's return to Paris meant. When he was asked to play in the Louvre before the King on 24 October 1658, the piece of the evening was, as it happened, *Nicomède*, and it was only as a tail-piece that Molière offered a farcical sketch, *Le Docteur amoureux*, which he introduced as one of those light entertainments that had procured for him some reputation in the provinces. Between that October evening and the triumph of *L'École des femmes* four years and two months later lies perhaps the chief dramatic innovation of the 1660s, nothing less than the attempt to make the comedy into the main attraction of a performance. There would at first sight seem to be nothing very revolutionary in this. Molière had *Le Menteur* before him, and the series of Corneille's comedies. But then *Le Docteur amoureux* was not that sort of comedy: it was something much nearer the low-class fare of the farce. It was something which, until Molière addressed himself to the task, no one had been able to convert into the staple ingredient of elegant entertainment.

We can see the steps by which Molière enlarged his appeal and his material. What we cannot follow is the process of decision whereby he eliminated alternatives. It may be that he fancied himself as a tragic actor, or that he hoped to modernize tragic diction. In *L'Étourdi* and *Le Dépit amoureux* he seems to have experimented with a five-act elegant comedy such as *Le Menteur*. But surely the success of *Les Précieuses ridicules* gave him other ideas. The plot of that short play was both simple and symbolic. That valets should impersonate masters, and succeed in hoodwinking girls from the provinces, is not profound. It may not even have been decent. What we know of the history and the background of the play suggests that it may have been much rougher, even to the point of slander, than the revised version that Molière supplied after the first fortnight's run, and which we now read. But to link the desire for culture with an underlying desire to avoid reality and to live in a world of make-believe, such as the novels of that day supplied, this goes deeper. This is something that opens the door to the old *esprit gaulois*, that bids fair to extend the domain of comedy into an almost Shakespearian horizon. If comedy can thus play off the affected, the romantic, the silly, and the vain, against the natural, the earthy, the real, then a new sort of play has been discovered, a play that may be dignified, artificial, complex, but will never lose sight of the natural, the physical, the earthbound. All this is foreshadowed in the *Précieuses ridicules*.

From the point of view of technique the next step after the *Précieuses* may well have been the most difficult: *Sganarelle, ou le Cocu imaginaire* was first given at the end of May 1660, and proved another success. It was a one-act comedy, but in verse. Thus a veil (is that the right expression?) of elegance and artifice is cast

over one of the homely figures of French farce. It starts at the point
where the *Précieuses* finish, with a diatribe against the way modern
girls are corrupted by novels. It deals with the misadventures of
a bourgeois and his wife, each suspicious of the other. It uses
the stock tricks, remarks overheard, couples surprised by a third
party, misunderstandings over a portrait. Nothing, one would
think, all that new, except the verve, the speed, and essentially
the language. It is in places the grand language of the serious
play:

> Et tu m'oses tenir de semblables discours
> — Et tu m'oses jouer de ces diables de tours.

In such a couplet the fusion of natural and theatrical speech is
easy to see: the first line might have come from a tragedy. But we
have only to remember that Molière acted the main part to see how
certain lines would come over with a quite new ring:

> C'est mon homme, ou plutôt c'est celui de ma femme
> Je ne suis point battant, de peur d'être battu
> Qu'il vaut mieux être encor cocu que trépassé
> Elles font la sottise et nous sommes les sots

If such a hybrid in one act were possible, why not in five? So in
February 1661 Molière put on his third experiment: *Don Garcie de
Navarre, ou Le Prince jaloux, comédie héroique en cinq actes*. This
time the public said No. The verse was splendid, but the complicated plot and Molière's natural diction must have seemed all
wrong. So he tried to compromise in three acts, and before the end
of the year produced *L'École des maris* and *Les Fâcheux*. The tragic
diction was not needed; neat observation and comic gesture helped
out the satire, and audiences were encouraging. So the final step
was possible, on 20 December 1662, with *L'École des femmes*. This
was such a success that even nowadays, for most people interested
in French theatre, 1662 means *L'École des femmes*. But for the
playgoer of 1662 it was probably not the play of the year. The Hôtel
put on tragedies by Boyer (*Polycrite*), by Thomas Corneille

D

(*Maximien*), by Mme de Villedieu (*Manlius Torquatus*, in which it was said that the Abbé d'Aubignac had the chief hand), by Gilbert (*Théagène*), and a one-act comedy by Poisson (*Le Baron de la Crasse*). The Court were probably more interested in a royal ballet, *Les Amours d'Hercule* by Benserade and Lully, literally royal, since both King and Queen took part. Perhaps the play of the year was to be seen at the Marais: *Sertorius* by Pierre Corneille, which, in the view of critics such as Chapelain, was as good as Corneille had often done in the past. This is the true context of Molière's first masterpiece. It might well form a subject for research.

We know the main source of the play, and any who can may read Scarron's absurd story of the Spaniard who trained a simple girl to be the perfect wife, who would have none of the qualities that might attract lovers. Molière cleverly combines this theme with another, probably from the *commedia dell'arte*, in which a young gallant confides in a bourgeois with two names, and thus at every step reveals to the suspicious Arnolphe what success he has had with Agnès. These sketchy *données* were enough for Molière to build his first full-length comic structure. He did it by making his bourgeois into a symbol, of narrowminded middle-class morality, a man for whom scandal is a worse enemy than an unhappy wife. With resource and method Arnolphe plans his scheme, finds the right girl and puts her in a convent, so that she may know nothing of the world and its ways. He hopes to be saved by her stupidity, and her *naïveté* is certainly extreme. It must have delighted the sophisticated audiences of the Palais Royal theatre. The scheme fails of course, since in her innocence and tactless directness she is quite charming, and attracts not only a lover but Arnolphe himself. The opposition of experience and artlessness is still one of the joys of the play. The action is carried by Arnolphe as central and ubiquitous character, and thus is under the direction of Molière himself, as it were, at every point. We may imagine how he could act the heavy husband reading to the bemused girl the famous maxims of marriage, and threatening her with all the torments of hell if she did not carry them out. The play shows the changes of her awakening, with a quiet, enchanting freshness, to a world in which people do not say what they mean, and give wrong meanings to what one says. The central point is a letter (in prose) which almost in itself opens a new domain for comedy:

> Since it is dawning on me that I have been kept in a state of ignorance, I am fearful of putting down anything which is not right and of saying more than I should. But in truth I know not what you have done to me. I know only that I am miserable at what they force me to do against you, that it would be the hardest thing in the world to do without you, and that I would be happy indeed to be yours. (III. 5)

One could not parallel, I think, this *naïveté* in plays of the time. Molière built his comedy on a temperamental opposition. The innocence of youth and inexperience is offset by the ponderous calculations of Arnolphe, which are careful to omit nothing, and in fact only omit common sense. That such a pedant should in the end turn lover had nothing pathetic about it in 1662. Molière took care that his acting should keep it on a note of absurdity, as we know from the discussion play, *La Critique de 'L'École des femmes'*, where one character objects to the new mixture of serious and absurd:

> And then there is this M. de la Souche, presented as a man of wit and in many things a sensible man; but in the fifth Act, surely he falls very low in vulgar (*comique*) overacting, as he makes plain to Agnes how passionately he loves her, with all the rolling of eyes, absurd sighing, and silly tears, which make everyone laugh? (Sc. vi)

Incidentally, the use of *comique* here suggests that midway area of low class domesticity, which it was precisely Molière's originality to explore.

Why did Molière's play touch off a quarrel comparable to that which had followed *Le Cid* twenty-five years previously? No doubt professional jealousy played its part, and no doubt the French are always ready for a battle of wits, but it seems clear that *L'École des femmes* gave its public a shock similar to that of *Le Cid*. Hindsight should enable us to appreciate that each play opened up possibilities of a dramatic form so far unsuspected. In essentials that form was the same, the form of the serious classical play, in which rhetoric was used to convey carefully chosen oppositions, refined to the point where drama consisted in the opposition itself, and not in anything that happened because of it. The best plays of Corneille are still able to give us this pleasure of contrasted attitudes and opposition. We have seen how impressive is Corneille's handling of fanaticism, for instance: his Polyeucte is the sort of man who is nerved to acts of daring because he can see only one side of a question. Molière's handling of a dramatic situation seems to me similar. These dramatists do not handle situations, they imagine, as poets, basic oppositions.

In the case of Molière, the plays in which he has done this are called *comédies de caractère*, an expression which some of us are reluctant to use because it conveys a suggestion of studies in psychology. To consider the greater comedies in such a light is to miss their greatness; *L'Avare* tells us little that is new about the psychology of avarice. It is a powerful dramatic struggle between the human elements in all of us, and that mixture of cupidity and fear, that shortsighted close-fistedness, which we may suppose to make up love of money. I think it may be said that in *L'École des femmes* Molière invented the *comédie de caractère*, in the sense of a play depending on a notion, a mania, an attitude, so extreme that its every encounter with the real world is a clash of forces as dramatic as any sequence of events. So I would agree with M. Jacques Guicharnaud, who devoted a special study to *Tartuffe, Le Misanthrope*, and *Dom Juan* as plays that were made possible by the break-through of 1662 to a new form of comedy.

The victory of *L'École des femmes* was worth celebrating, and worth discussing, and it is no accident that the play evoked from its author two dramatic comments on his art. The first of these we have already mentioned, *La Critique*; this slight play is a landmark in dramatic criticism. In accents that recall Corneille it insists that dramatic rules are subordinate to the pleasure of the audience. A play is written to rule so that it may give more, and purer, pleasure.

You cut a pretty figure with your rules, which only confuse the uninitiated and give us all wrong ideas all the time. To go by you, the rules of art would seem to be the world's greatest mysteries, yet they are only a few gentle comments, made from the angle of common sense, as to what may hinder our pleasure; and common sense is the same now as it was with Horace and Aristotle. I wonder if the great rule is not the need to

give pleasure, and if a play that does so is not thereby well constructed.
(Sc. vi)

It is a plea *pro domo* and does not go to the heart of the matter,
although it makes excellent material for discussion, and underlines
the primacy of the dramatic element, as the element which grips an
audience.

One other critical point made in the *Critique* seems to be of even
greater importance. A lady asks whether a good comedy is not as
difficult to achieve as a tragedy. To another this is absurd: 'il y a
une grande différence de toutes ces bagatelles à la beauté des pièces
sérieuses.' But it gives Molière the chance to defend his art in the
person of Dorante:

Indeed, Madam, and for comedy you could safely imagine it even more
difficult to create. It is easier, methinks, to proffer high sentiments, mock
at Fortune, or defy the gods than it is to understand the comic side of men,
and to make people's faults into stage entertainment. You are free to say
what you like about heroes, for they need not resemble anyone; you may
give free rein to your fancy, and even leave the truth in order to suggest
the marvellous. But when you are describing ordinary people you must
keep to real life. Your sketches have to be credible, . . . it is, in fact, an odd
business to make decent people laugh. (Sc. vi)

This is better criticism than we could find in any of the critics
considered in the last chapter. It is the charter-deed of the new
comedy, and Boileau had only to reread it to formulate the precepts
of his *Art poétique*. But it is unlikely that even Molière knew how
strange was the enterprise he had embarked on. Within the space of
ten years he was to supply all sorts of comic entertainment, for all
sorts of occasions, but based, I think, on the two principles enun-
ciated by Dorante: that the characters should be lifelike, and that
they should give pleasure to honest men. The two aims appear
contradictory. The talent of a La Rochefoucauld could not possibly
satisfy both. Of all Molière's contemporaries only La Fontaine
appeared to be able to amuse and to be true to life. If we could
understand and explain how Molière did it, we should have defined
his genius.

For our present purpose it is sufficient to repeat that perhaps the

most notable event on the Paris stage in the 1660s was the achievement of a new comedy in *L'École des femmes*, and the definition
of that achievement in *La Critique*. The quarrel of *Le Cid* may
have raised as much dust as that of 1662–3, but it resulted in no
such novelty of dramatic theory.

Little attention has been given to the actual conditions of production in this most important decade. M. Bray is the only scholar
who has worked out what one might call the economics of Molière's
company. Plays were hard to come by, the public was small; each
of the three Paris theatres seems to have had a struggle to keep
above water and to guarantee its company anything like a living
wage. In fact there was no wage: the takings were divided, and in
the case of most plays they soon sank so low that the life of a play
was often very short. Let us look at the receipts of the 1664–5 season,
as M. Bray presents them. Because of the interdict on *Tartuffe*, the
only Molière comedies to bring in much money were *La Princesse
d'Élide* and *Le Festin de Pierre*. The company put on *Cinna* (twice)
and *Sertorius* (five times), Racine's first tragedy (twenty), two
Scarron comedies, and five farces. The failure of *Tartuffe* to bring in
money resulted in the 'part' or actor's share of the year's takings
falling to 3,000 livres (roughly, perhaps, 20,000 francs). The following season was nearly as bad. The death of Anne of Austria meant
that the theatre had to be closed for most of January and February.
Fourteen plays were put on in seven weeks, including eight
comedies of Molière, whose illness faced his company with disaster.

The history of *Tartuffe* tells us a good deal about the problems
of an actor-manager in Paris of the 1660s. It effectively destroys, to
begin with, the old picture of Molière as a reasonable, middle-of-
the-road man, who took the view of the *raisonneurs* in his plays.
Such a man would have given up the struggle to put on a play so
offensive to authority. Only a man of extreme force of character,
courage, and persistence could have fought a five-year fight as
Molière did. Many must have thought, and told him, that he was
crazy to hope for public performance. Three versions are known:
the first (probably complete in three acts) is the comedy played at
Versailles on 12 May 1664, and denied public performance. The
second, entitled *L'Imposteur*, in five acts, was put on for a single

night at the Palais Royal (5 August 1667). Its content is known from the *Lettre sur 'L'Imposteur'* published soon after. The third is the play as we know it, performed at the Palais Royal on 5 February 1669. By then it was, of course, a money-spinner: it was put on forty times in two years.

This stormy history has affected the reputation of the play. So much has been said about it as controversial and satiric that modern readers have failed to take it as a comedy. Professors gravely discuss which character may properly be called funny, and great actors have played the main part with various shades of satire. It comes, therefore, as a relief to find a scholar writing that 'si le spectateur du 17e siècle m'assure que Tartuffe se montrait ridicule, j'aime mieux l'en croire que de conjecturer avec Michaut qu'il ne l'était pas.' If we think of Molière playing Orgon (and directing *Tartuffe*) as he played *L'École des femmes*, we cannot think that his public was left in any doubt about the comedy of the play. Whatever the undertones or implications, they were asked to watch a man whose common sense had deserted him, for excellent reasons of piety, opposite another man who, like Arnolphe, had a scheme, a clever scheme, but having the fatal flaw of neglecting the sensual element in people, and most particularly in himself. Is this not the new comedy in magnificent guise? Gestures and attitudes are as if copied from life; yet ugly qualities, even sins, are in this play refreshing to contemplate, because they are seen in a context of the whole man. The point about Tartuffe is not his sensuality but his folly: an impostor who lets his instincts ruin his plan is an absurdity.

For a man who had tasted the hostility of the Church, to stage a play about an atheist, while *Tartuffe* was still banned, was surely a very foolish act. *Dom Juan* had only fifteen performances, and was never revived in Molière's lifetime. The affinity with Arnolphe is still perceptible. The atheist is presented not as a vicious figure so much as a narrow-minded man, who has the preposterous notion that he can dispense with all obligation towards other people. (Again the portrait is life-like, when compared with some contemporary French aristocrats.) He therefore despises his servant, insults his father, deceives his tradesman, promises marriage to several girls, scorns the Scripture, and refuses to acknowledge any belief. He goes to hell, of course, and without that end to the story Molière could not have given it comic treatment. The play that Molière has made from the legend is not only delightful for the opposition between master and servant (the nearest Molière ever came to Cervantes) but is hinged on the paradox that an all-too-human man cannot set aside human obligations.

As one reflects on these successive productions it appears that the years 1664–6 were the period of Molière's most intense production. To have conceived *Tartuffe* (even in its first form) and *Dom Juan* and *Le Misanthrope* all within three years is by any standard an impressive achievement. The formula of *La Critique* held good for them all. They were brilliantly lifelike; they showed the human condition as we know it to be. And yet they were refreshing, in that folly was not shown up as wrong so much as exposed as self-destructive. Alceste's pride is often found in reformers: it is brilliant dramatic use of misanthropy to show a man thinking that all the world has gone wrong, except himself. To see these great plays in their context, as this chapter tries to do, we must remind ourselves that they were accompanied by lighter pieces: *L'Amour médecin*, *Le Médecin malgré lui*, *Le Bourgeois Gentilhomme*, *George Dandin*, which, as Diderot said, shows no less skill than those that we consider greater, and no different view of comedy. And they were played on a stage which still gave to tragedy pride of place in most performances.

Here too the 1660s see a great change. If such a play as *Sertorius* may rank with the best of Corneille, its successor *Sophonisbe* called forth strong contemporary criticism and reads now as a very imperfect dramatic structure. But there were signs of new talent in the first two plays of Racine, *La Thébaïde* in 1664 and *Alexandre* in 1665. Racine confirmed the signs with two marvellous tragic creations: *Andromaque* in 1667 and *Britannicus* in 1669. Both were successful; both were shown hostility by contemporary writers, partly, no doubt, owing to the scornful prefaces which preceded the plays in the first edition.

If one asks what Racine offered to the playgoers of the 1660s that his contemporaries had not given them, we can find the answer, I suggest, by rereading Molière's views on realism in *La Critique*, quoted above. Realism has replaced heroics; the kings and queens of tragedy are people who share the common lot and who are not superior to it. What is kingly, in the Cornelian sense, about Pyrrhus, or Nero, except their language? What, then, delights us in seeing great persons defeated? This is a question that still awaits a considered answer. It may be the judicious (Dryden's word for Corneille) fusion of human attitudes: dignity, pride, passion, suffering, lunacy . . . all these are focused and brought into play in *Andromaque* by a few exquisitely chosen motives. It may be the tragic flash itself that lights up the abyss of horror surrounding apparently simple decisions. Nero is shown by Racine as master of the world, yet unable to make up his mind, and justifiably so, since his independence was bound up with a career of crime. It may have been no accident that Racine's now famous definition of tragedy occurs in his first Preface to *Britannicus*, a play which when compared with others of its time has indeed 'une action simple, chargée de peu de matière', but which is entirely 'soutenue par les intérêts, les sentiments et les passions des personnages'.

Yet we must not hide the fact that while Racine's first two plays fit without difficulty into the dramatic production of their time, his two following tragedies seem with equal ease to transcend that pattern, to throw off the limitations of a complicated plot and a false rhetoric; thus they have kept for now 300 years that capacity to please which the early plays almost immediately lost.

It may be that the features we like to call Racinian are found in his first plays. There is symbolism in plenty in *La Thébaïde*, and a recent investigation has seen it as 'clustering around the concept of disrelation', the rupture of links between families and persons, the isolation of kingship, so that a throne elevates and engulfs the same person:

Ce trône fut toujours un dangereux abîme.

The tragic possibilities of power may be envisaged in such a play, but they are brought much closer to us in *Andromaque*. The difference between these two plays may not at first be clear to a foreigner, or on a first reading. Both are couched in an artificial form of speech, both deal with figures of ancient legend, yet *La Thébaïde*, whatever techniques we invent to explain it, will, I think, remain just a French classical tragedy, while *Andromaque* appears to be one of the world's masterpieces, a reason in itself why French classical tragedies should merit interest, performance, study.

Here again, the scholar can do little more than discern a difference: he cannot assign a convincing reason for it. As I try to analyse *Andromaque*, I find that the mastery and the poetry first come home to me in the great fourth scene of the opening Act, when Pyrrhus the victor attempts to use his hold on his captive's son in order to force her love. The dialogue is vibrant, psychologically true (though not to my mind very subtle), intensely dramatic. Yet it is as far removed as possible from historical reality or likelihood. It is conducted with French elegance and politeness:

> Me cherchiez-vous, Madame?
> Un espoir si charmant me serait-il permis? (259)

and by the conqueror with all the *langage precieux* of the 1660s, which delighted to dwell on the 'wounds' of love:

> Vaincu, chargé de fers, de regrets consumé
> Brûlé de plus de feux que je n'en allumai (320)

But he is face to face with one for whom these words are not polite conceits, they are literal and searing truth; his prisoner is really 'vaincue', 'chargée de fers'; she is terrified by the memory not of the 'burning' pangs of love but of the burning city in which her husband perished. So when clumsily pressed to be 'merciful' she flashes out in verse that suggests (but only suggests) torment of spirit:

> Troie, Hector, contre vous révoltent-ils son âme?
> Aux cendres d'un époux doit-elle enfin sa flamme?
> Et quel époux encore. Ah, souvenir cruel. . . . (359)

Andromaque covers in event little of the story of Homer's Andromache. The murder of Pyrrhus by Orestes at the behest of the outraged Hermione is, as Racine claims in a preface, almost its entire subject. As in Corneille, events are replaced by attitudes, which at times have a ferocity and a lucidity denied to events.

Almost the ultimate in concentration is reached when Hermione admits her desperate desire both to kill and to preserve the lover who has injured her, yet without whom she cannot live:

> Qu'il meure, puisqu'enfin il a dû le prévoir,
> Et puisqu'il m'a forcée enfin à le vouloir.
> A le vouloir? Hé quoi, c'est donc moi qui l'ordonne? (1421)

It may be such lines that have made people admire the psychological depth of French classical tragedy, and in particular of Racine. I prefer to think with Brémond and Maulnier that we are not reading psychology, but poetry, devised by 'le plus humain des poètes'.

Within two years of *Andromaque* Racine performed a similar miracle, as indeed he was to do six times over, within eight years. He had found in Tacitus a subject which allowed him, as *Andromaque* had done and as *Berenice* was to do, the most severe limitation of incident, or, putting it the other way round, the utmost concentration of interest on a central issue. The issue, in this case, was in the mind of an Emperor: whether or not to commit what would in the end be the first of many crimes. *Britannicus* seems to me a tragedy powerfully focused on this notion of independence. One might call the play a study of the choices confronting Nero who, being master of the world, can in theory do as he likes. But in fact he can only have Junia at the cost of offending Agrippina, the mother whom he fears and who will not give up her hold over him. He would like to follow the advice of Burrhus and be a strong ruler, but his other counsellor Narcissus has the more seductive words. In the end he murders his rival Britannicus, but cynically, as though exhausted in the attempt to find a way out, a way to independence otherwise than through crime. Our interest is intense, in motive, in the complexities which surround decision. At the end we ask, as at the close of a sublimated detective story: who was it, really, who caused that crime? What is it, essentially, that makes a responsible person? In fact, what is freedom?

7
The Seventies

THIS decade should be the peak of the story. The last four plays of
Molière, five of Racine at his greatest, is not that enough to suggest
that the 1670s rival and surpass even the 1660s in classical achievement? Close study gives a different impression. We have only to
put these well-known works back in their context to see how
fragile is this thing we have come to call classicism. Molière after
Tartuffe is a broken man, with three years to live. Racine achieves
more success from the public than popularity within his profession.
His plays are exceptions, in their severity, in their classical simplicity. The three Paris theatres put on many more sensational plays,
comedies by Hauteroche, Poisson, de Visé, machine-plays like de
Visé's *Amours de Vénus et d'Adonis* (1670) or Thomas Corneille's
Triomphe des dames (1676). The new taste was for ballet, spectacle,
opera, admirably catered for by Quinault and Lully in collaboration:
Thésée (1674), *Isis* (1677), *Proserpine* (1680), *Le Triomphe de
l'amour* (1681), *Persée* (1682), *Phaeton* (1683), *Roland Furieux*
(1685); and by Thomas Corneille working with Fontenelle (*Psyche*
(1679), *Bellérophon* (1679)), and with de Visé (*La Devineresse*
(1679)). This production was in part a reflexion of the king's personal taste. He preferred to have music in plays, and chose the
subject of several operas, then called 'tragédies lyriques'. Of the
Roland Furieux we are told two things which suggest a change in
royal taste: 'On travaille à un nouvel opera dont Roland le Furieux
fera le sujet, et c'est encore le Roi qui a choisi, et marqué cette
matière à M. Quinaut et à M. Lulli . . .'; and in another document:

'on eut à Versailles la première représentation de l'opéra de Roland, qu'on devait avoir à l'avenir seulement une fois par semaine . . . le Roi déclara que ces sortes de spectacles l'ennuyaient quand il les voyait représenter si souvent' (both documents given by Mélèse, *Répertoire*, 178).

What should we set on the other side of the picture? The fact that Racine was appreciated as an outstanding author, as indeed was Molière. A contemporary refers to Racine as 'cet illustre génie, favorisé des puissances, admiré du peuple et approuvé des savants', and on this judgement M. Picard comments thus:

He is favoured by all parties. His taste for the classics, for august literature, gives him distinction in addition to his own, and gets him known as learned. It is a rare thing for a writer to be not only in fashion but to be appreciated as not for the generality. His strategic position half-way between the Court and the world of letters makes of him a judge in matters of taste.

(R. PICARD, *La Carrière de Jean Racine* (1956), p. 253)

It would seem, indeed, that the esteem, among the discerning few no doubt, for Racine and Molière altered the image of what one meant by an author. M. Picard quotes (p. 64) the opinion of Primi Visconti in 1678: 'En France on n'estime que les titres de guerre; ceux des lettres et de toute autre profession sont méprisés. . . . L'on considère comme vil l'homme de qualité qui sait écrire' (op. cit., p. 64).

When contemporaries spoke of Racine or Molière as 'illustre' they had no thought of separating them, save in capacity, from the theatrical production of their day. We, who no longer know that production, can only judge their survival value, which is independent of the context in which they first appeared. It may seem tiresome to repeat the point, so let us take an example, and suppose we were in Paris in the month of November 1670. We should be able to see *Bérénice* at the Hôtel de Bourgogne from the 21st onwards (for at least thirty performances, said Racine in his Preface). We should see at the Palais Royal *Le Misanthrope* and *George Dandin*, neither playing to capacity, and on 23 November *Le Bourgeois Gentilhomme*, already played before the Court at Chambord and

Saint-Germain. And we should see it alternately until mid-March with Corneille's tragedy *Tite et Bérénice*. We should hear the talk of the town as to how it came about that Corneille and Racine should have treated the same subject. We should, if we stayed on in Paris, hear of a *Critique de 'Bérénice'* by the Abbé de Villars, written, it appears, before Racine's play was performed, and available in print early in 1671. We should a few weeks later read a defence of Racine by Subligny, and not long after that Racine's own defence in the Preface to his published play. The effect of all this would no doubt be that we should consider the connections and similarities between the plays, note which actors played parts in more than one of them; and we should probably not get the feeling of a modern reader that one of the plays was comedy, the others tragedy, or that one, *Bérénice,* was so impressive that it was likely to be famous, while *Tite et Bérénice* would be forgotten. We might well feel that all these plays about ancient Rome gave us much the same sort of fare, and ask ourselves whether it was the acting, or even the reputation of an actress, that made the difference to our pleasure.

Similarly in 1672 we should watch Thomas Corneille's *Ariane* after seeing Racine's *Bajazet,* and then see *Les Femmes savantes* and (some months later) Corneille's *Pulchérie*, after it had been read in a salon before the Cardinal de Retz. After that, a tragedy adapted by Boursault from *La Princesse de Clèves*. So one could go on. The *Répertoire* drawn up by M. Mélèse enables us to see with what proximity these varied shows, all of which had some title to classical form, stood to each other, and to the small circle of actors and the still small public. As M. Schlumberger has expressed it:

Would Corneille have taken up the theatre again, had it not been that Henrietta of England urged him to do so? It is said that he was unaware of the dangerous competition he would meet. But in the Paris of those days, little more than a large village, it would have been an extraordinarily well-kept secret for plans to remain unknown from one coterie to another.

(JEAN SCHLUMBERGER, *Plaisir à Corneille*, p. 241)

In this kind of setting, what should we look for in Molière's last plays? Some no doubt sought in them a lesson of manners or a warning against pedants or charlatans. Even so intelligent a man as Father Rapin found moral lessons in *Les Femmes savantes*: 'Il y a dans cette comédie des caractères rares et d'une grande instruction pour une jeune personne; car le ridicule des femmes qui font vanité de ce qu'elles savent y est bien exprimé (Mélèse, op. cit., p. 151).

A feature which must have caused pleasure in the theatre was Molière's astonishing power to imagine *naïveté*, again something which would please an audience that hated to think itself naïve. His picture of Jourdain (a man competent in his own sphere but anxious to do everything to get out of it, to do as great people do) surely gave much delight from the start. He is obviously silly, and essentially likable: his pleasure in study, in the discovery that he has spoken prose for forty years, in learning how to kill a man by logic, all these on a level: 'Ah, la belle chose que de savoir quelque chose.' A companion figure to Jourdain is Chrysale, the delight of *Les Femmes savantes*. A homely man who goes in fear of his wife, who finds the jargon of the learned ladies no substitute for good house-keeping ('Je vis de bonne soupe et non de beau langage'), whose love of peace and of brother body ('Guenille si l'on veut, ma guenille m'est chère') makes him dread his masterful partner: he is unable even to put up a defence of the servant sacked for bad grammar. These are the delights of *Les Femmes savantes*, more than the ostensible subject. The play turns out to be comedy first and satire second. It uses the classical form to perfection: nothing jars, nothing is far-fetched or irrelevant. The verse keeps the tone just far enough away from the everyday to convey attitudes in conflict; not disastrous conflict, as in a tragedy, but basic temperamental conflict, which we watch with satisfaction because we are on both sides: our vision is enlarged by the delicate presentation of extremes.

In these late plays Molière seems to me to be still working on the lines laid down in *La Critique* and the *Lettre sur 'L'Imposteur'*. They are in fact studies of the absurd, pictures of folly, but imagined against a background of that reason of which the folly is the opposite. It is difficult to put this point as well as he put it: 'Pour connaître ce ridicule il faut connaître la raison dont il signifie le défaut et voir en quoi elle consiste.' The implications of this we have already treated, but for the moment let us see that this double principle—the concept of folly, shown beside the good sense which is the counterpart of the folly—is worked out in a tight dramatic structure, pleasing because transparent and easy to follow, an achievement which Pierre Corneille, for all his dramatic skill, hardly ever reached. Let us hear how M. Reynier takes to pieces the structural mechanism of *Les Femmes savantes*: 'Without claiming to say how a great work came to be, we can make a guess as to how Molière saw his characters group in his mind . . . women claiming competence in both science and letters . . . a topsy-turvy household, where the weak husband is frightened of the masterful wife . . . young lovers whose path does not run smooth . . . two sisters . . . two suitors' (*Les Femmes savantes*, p. 75).

André Malraux once said of his fiction: 'Je ne pars pas des personnages, je pars de la situation.' This might explain the power of plays in which we have accustomed ourselves to look only for people. The clever dramatist is he who can imagine a situation that shall show up people, as being not only credible but akin to us.

Molière's later plays seem to me the perfection of *raillerie*, that quality of perceiving the incongruous, a quality much admired in the seventeenth century; its greatest exponents, such as Richelieu and Mme de Montespan, were noted for the cruelty of their wit. It is commonly imagined that Molière exposed pedantry and folly by showing how silly they were. But that is half the story. Richelieu had a biting wit and was so powerful that he need not fear giving offence. Molière tempered the wit with the power of art, which allowed him to see, and to show, folly in the round, as part of the human condition. This is why the *folie de grandeur* of Jourdain is both puerile and pleasant, why the bluestockings, for all their wit, do not steal the show. This is why Argan, again, in the last dramatic creation it was given Molière to complete, is shown as a man whose illness consists less in physical disorder than in superstition and fear of his doctors. To see in *Le Malade imaginaire* a satire of the Paris Faculty of Medicine or of the medical profession is to single out an important, but artistically a secondary, feature. The charlatans are opposed, as dramatically they must be, by their victim, but the encounter has the sting taken out of it by the suggestion that Argan need only remain their victim as long as he makes no use of the common sense which is in all of us.

Such delicate fantasies seem far removed from the later plays of Corneille, yet it was the same actor (La Grange) who played Tartuffe and Attila and Tite. Tragedy used the same classical form of rhetorical exploration of dilemmas, choices open to the great, of the clash between character and event, will and power. It seems a pity, when one reads *Tite et Bérénice*, that it had to clash with Racine's powerful play, and thus bear for ever the ticket of a second best. For Corneille has his old skill of finding superb formulations of the classical attitudes. The paradox of being Roman emperor must have been an actor's joy to express in a most commanding tone. Burrhus, for example: 'Ce n'est plus votre fils, c'est le maître du monde.' But is this less impressive, from *Tite et Bérénice?* 'Maître de l'univers, a-t-il un maître à craindre?' The master himself is not in Corneille's play as subtle as Néron, but again, would not the acting, in the conditions of that time, be just as impressive?

> Pour envoyer l'effroi sous l'un et l'autre pôle
> Je n'ai qu'à faire un pas et hausser la parole.
>
> Maître de l'univers sans l'être de moi-même,
> Je suis le seul rebelle à ce pouvoir suprême.

Racine was not the only one who knew the effect on the stage of the 'disorder' of passion disturbing the order of reason:

(Tite)   Peut-être en ce moment que toute ma raison
           Ne saurait sans désordre entendre son beau nom. (369)

(Domitie) Je m'emporte et mes sens interdits
           Impriment leur désordre en tout ce que je dis. (701)

Mme de Sévigné was always moved by this rhetoric; one feels that in defending the later plays of Corneille she is always hoping that the master will somehow 'do it again':

Corneille a lu (au Cardinal de Retz) une comédie qui sera jouée dans quelque temps, et qui fait souvenir des anciennes. Je suis folle de Corneille; il nous redonnera encore *Pulchérie* où l'on verra encore

> la main qui crayonna
> La mort du grand Pompée et l'amour de Cinna.

Il faut que tout cède au génie.

Even our contempories find some sign of genius in the role of
Martian, created in the same year as Acomat, and into which some
have read the regrets of the ageing poet himself:

> Je pouvais aspirer au cœur le mieux placé
> Mais hélas j'étais jeune et ce temps est passé
> Qu'avec, s'il faut le dire, une espèce de rage . . .
> Je m'attachais sans crainte à servir la princesse,
> Fier de mes cheveux blancs, et fort de ma faiblesse
> Et quand je ne pensais qu'à remplir mon devoir,
> Je devenais amant sans m'en apercevoir.
>
> J'ai caché si longtemps l'ennui qui me dévore
> Qu'en dépit que j'en aie, enfin il s'évapore.
> L'aigreur en diminue à te le raconter.

I think I would rather have heard Corneille read these lines in
the presence of Retz and Mme de Sévigné than have listened to
La Grange reciting them, to what Bayle says was a thin house.

It was like Corneille to finish with a flourish. A critic of our day
calls *Suréna* (December 1674, three months after *Iphigénie*) 'very
nearly a great play'. Yet again the well-known situation places
kings and generals before Montaigne's choice of 'l'utile et l'honnête'.
A princess, Eurydice, is prepared to take her devotion to the limit:

> Le trépas à vos yeux me semblerait trop doux
> Et je n'ai pas encore assez souffert pour vous.
> Je veux qu'un noir chagrin à pas lents me consume
> Qu'il me fasse à longs traits goûter son amertume.
> Je veux, sans que la mort ose me secourir,
> Toujours aimer, toujours souffrir, toujours mourir.

Suréna himself is prepared to dispense with immortality for one
crowded hour of glorious life:

> Que tout meure avec moi, Madame, que m'importe
> Qui foule après ma mort la terre qui me porte? . . .
> Quand nous avons perdu le jour qui nous éclaire
> Cette sorte de vie est bien imaginaire,
> Et le moindre moment d'un bonheur souhaité
> Vaut mieux qu'une si froide et vaine éternité.

These lines are chosen by M. Jean Schlumberger to close his anthology, because they illustrate, in their baroque splendour, what he calls Corneille's 'sunset': 'One might expect a variety of tone, harsh and gentle, to appear in the last plays, above all such as would make a grand farewell to the heroic world and enable Corneille to round off his career' (*Plaisir à Corneille*, p. 270). Yet, with respect, it is not as a sounding board that we should take leave of a dramatist who was much more than a rhetorician. His true glory was to fashion, almost single-handed, a form of dramatic poetry which, by one of the great coincidences of literature, was made ready to the hand of one of the great tragic poets of the world. Without Corneille, Racine is unthinkable. Modern research seems only to have confirmed Lanson's judgement: 'Avant lui, notre théâtre classique n'existait pas; par lui, il a existé.'

The first critic of Racine's *Bérénice* found it effeminate, sentimental, and above all empty: '. . . toute la pièce matière d'une scène'. In reply Subligny defended the vigour of the verse, and Racine, in his Preface, claimed that his subject was not only a famous piece of history but dramatic to a high degree: 'je l'ai trouvée très propre pour la théâtre par la violence des passions qu'elle y pouvait exciter.' The phrase was perhaps ill-chosen, and might easily have been picked up by Bossuet, who was to argue that the theatre was immoral because it did precisely this: it excited passion rather than purified it. Racine went on to compare the farewell of Bérénice to that of Dido in Vergil (thus going back to some of the earliest Renaissance attempts at classical tragedy), and to show that the excitement of passion of which he was thinking was not unhealthy but a necessary part of tragic pleasure. Would not Corneille have agreed with almost every clause of Racine's now famous definition, except perhaps the last?

Ce n'est point une nécessité qu'il y ait du sang et des morts dans une tragédie: il suffit que l'action en soit grande, que les acteurs en soient héroïques, que les passions y soient excitées, et que tout s'y ressente de cette tristesse majestueuse qui fait tout le plaisir de la tragédie.

Mr Fergusson has analysed the symbolism and the power of this play so well that there is no need to say much here (*Idea of a*

Theater, paperback edn. pp. 54–80). For us the main difficulty in studying *Bérénice* has to do less with the nature of the subject than with the technical skill whereby the poet constructs an action filling five acts, out of what would seem to be a single sentence of Suetonius. If we are justified in thinking that Racine was writing for a generation who were tired of heroics and the *invraisemblable*, who had been trained by Molière to expect dramatic subjects to be lifelike, human, easy to imagine, rather than complex and out of the ordinary ('il n'y a que le vraisemblable qui touche dans une tragédie'), then this is a crucial point. Here I think Mr Fergusson can help us: 'The art by which Racine makes his story seem to move, though a most difficult technical achievement, is fundamentally very simple. He withholds until the very end, from one or more of his three main characters, some crucial fact of that character's situation, and so forces them all to explore every logical possibility, and ring all the changes upon hope and despair' (op. cit., p. 44).

This implies that in *Bérénice* Racine has invented a form of tragedy in which the situation does not change. Our suspense is caused by the characters' gradual discovery of the real situation. This is surely the kind of play which *Horace* and *Polyeucte* suggested. What may look like a sequence of events leading to murder or to martyrdom is powerful and attractive in so far as it assembles the elements whereby a tragic situation may be fully seized. Racine would thus appear as fulfilling the Cornelian programme. He conveys suspense, not by unexpected events but by showing an emotion so intense that it cannot bring itself to speak the word of departure:

> Résolu d'accomplir ce cruel sacrifice
> J'y voulus préparer la triste Bérénice
> Mais par où commencer? Vingt fois depuis huit jours
> J'ai voulu devant elle en ouvrir le discours
> Et dès le premier mot ma langue embarrassée
> Dans ma bouche vingt fois a demeuré glacée. (471–6)

A recent London performance confirmed my feeling that here we have a dramatic form used to perfection. Such a play makes full use, at last, after years of experiment by many authors, of a form discovered and fitfully grasped by Corneille. The usual effect of a tragedy upon us is that we are sensitive to disaster, overtaking people engaged in some great undertaking. French classical tragedy so rediscovers the steps whereby people become conscious of threat and danger that we who watch find ourselves also entering into the gradual process of recognition. We, not only they, are in fact discovering tragic possibilities.

It seems to have been a tale told by an ambassador that gave Racine the material for his next experiment in this kind of tragedy. *Bajazet* (5 January 1672) shocked its first critics by its savagery and Hamlet-like ending of general slaughter. The situation on which it is built has seemed to some too repulsive for a classical tragedy. A slave who confronts a prince with the choice of marriage or death is not edifying. As Racine explained in a second Preface, he has chosen a theme from Turkish history because of 'le mépris qu'ils font de la vie'. But the 'events' of the play are not its real events. The hero has no difficulty in rejecting blackmail, and he dies, we assume, a hero's death when he walks through a door in the knowledge that his murderers are on the other side. The tragic pity is concentrated on the slave, another Hermione in her passionate pursuit of what she must and cannot have. She gradually comes to realize (and we who watch take the same journey) that her passion is absurd, without meaning, since her only weapon is to kill what gives her life its meaning:

> Je te donne, cruel, des armes contre moi
> Sans doute et je devais rentenir ma faiblesse,
> Tu vas en triompher. Qui, je te le confesse,
> J'affectais à tes yeux une fausse fierté
> De toi dépend ma joie et ma felicité.
> De ma sanglante mort ta mort sera suivie. (552–7)

The year of *Bajazet* is the year of *Les Femmes savantes*. I find no unfitness in the conjunction. Both plays use the classical form to illumine implications of life in a civilized society, both explore the limits and the inconsequence of desire. Both continue to give pleasure, the one in the comic mode, the other in the tragic. We are wrong if we assume that the comic pleasure, just because it is comic, is more superficial than the other.

Racine had some trouble in constructing his next play, out of material in Appian and Plutarch. His Preface to *Mithridate* again rebuts the charge that he has altered history. The patient work of Gustave Rudler has shown how thin was the ice on which the poet trod: 'Confondre en un point du temps les années 90, 71 et 63, ressusciter deux personnes, vieillir l'une, rajeunir l'autre, pour leur permettre de s'aimer, il appelle cela, bénignement, rapprocher quelques événements par le droit que donne la poésie' (Blackwell edition (1943), p. x). Our withers are unwrung, by the alterations as by the defence. What should interest us is his desire to create a tragic subject. We shall find it bears close resemblance to the subject of *Bajazet*. Once again we are shown physical power, faced by defenceless dignity. Mithridate has spent his life in harrying Rome and has even mastered the effects of poison. But he meets his match in thinking he can order a girl to love him. When she refuses to do so, all his weapons are blunted, all his warrior's cunning is of no avail, since to kill Monime would almost amount to taking his own life. Like Roxane, Mithridate is slowly, in the course of elaborately arranged encounters, made aware of the existence of a moral universe, and of the limits, nay the absurdity, of physical power:

> Et le tombeau, Seigneur, est moins triste pour moi
> Que le lit d'un époux qui m'a fait cet outrage,
> Qui s'est acquis sur moi ce cruel avantage. (1350-2)

Is not this encounter as baroque and sentimental as anything in Corneille? But it was clearly to the taste of its public, and it allowed a full measure of tragic pity. We may not like the figure of Mithridate, but his acknowledgement of defeat is splendid:

> O Monime, o mon fils, inutile courroux . . .
> J'ai su par une longue et pénible industrie
> Des plus mortels venins prévenir la furie.
> Ah, qu'il eût mieux valu, plus sage et plus heureux,*
> Et repoussant les traits d'un amour dangereux,
> Ne pas laisser remplir d'ardeurs empoisonnées
> Un cœur déjà glacé par le froid des années. (1409-)

---

* Note that the minor stresses, at which an actor would pause, occur after the first, sixth and eighth syllables of this line. See below, p. 120.

We now pass to Racine's most enigmatic contribution to the stage in the 1670s: *Iphigénie*. It was his greatest success, played over forty times, and the criticisms levelled against it only served to evoke testimony to the extraordinary emotion ('une infinité de larmes') which it called forth. On the other hand, it is today the least regarded and most rarely played of all Racine's greater tragedies. No one has explained either the immediate success or the ultimate decline of the play. Both structure and language seem to show the poet in full exercise of his powers. As before, the characters are made to enter gradually into full realization of their peril. The emotional centre of the play would seem to be the distraught figure of the king, Agamemnon, convinced by the gods' messenger that the only way to bring his army home is to sacrifice his daughter. Yet his chief general Achilles demands her in marriage and is prepared to mutiny if refused. The human cost to a father of bringing death upon his innocent daughter finally persuades him to disobey the gods. Thereupon Achilles does revolt, but another victim is found. This most dramatic action is made to turn around the two meanings of the word *autel*, which is both the place of wedding, desired by Iphigénie, and the place of sacrifice, feared by her father:

> Verra-t-on à l'autel votre heureuse famille?
> . . . Vous y serez, ma fille.

Judgement on such a play has been made more difficult by recent research. M. Jasinski has found so many contemporary parallels to the action that he has no doubt of its application to the Profession of Louise de la Vallière and the revolt of Lauzun and the destitution of three marshals of the Army. All these events are known to have caused anxiety or anguish to the King. 'Dès lors, tout s'éclaire' (R. Jasinski, *Vers le vrai Racine*, ii. 246). It is, I think, reasonable to admit the force of the parallels with events at the French Court, and to think that Racine, who was much closer to them than we are, had them in mind while he was working out his play. But this is something very different from suggesting that the play was an allegory, and that all becomes clear if we imagine Racine to be writing about a spectacular contemporary sacrifice. Perhaps Racine's plays have connections with events around him more than we have liked to think. But to enforce rather than to suggest parallels is, in the end, to make matters more obscure, not clearer.

One cannot help feeling that something other than Court sensations impelled Racine to rival Euripides. Iphigénie is Racine's return to myth. In a sense this was happening all around him. Machine-plays, operas, ballet, all offered images of Cadmus, Jupiter, Alcestis to their public. Racine's attitude to myth is in austere contrast to such fripperies. For the first time since *La Thébaïde* he meditates a play which involves gods as well as men, in which the final decisions are taken by gods and not understood by men. Professor Vinaver sees this as a logical development of Racine's poetic:

> We need only to restore *Iphigénie* and *Phèdre* to the underlying pattern of Racinian poetry to sense at once that they fall into their logical place. His search for the tragic . . . could not but bring Racine back to legend, to the hard core of ancient themes, to the wide spaces of the Greek myths. . . . This fate, which is outside man and beyond his command, this dark mystery to which man seeks in vain an answer, this is a part of the play from its opening scene.
>
> (*Racine et la poésie tragique*, p. 81)

The central role, as Vinaver reminds us, is that of Agamemnon, a man, a ruler, and a father, called upon to take human, even political, decisions in a context of mystery and divine command. Thus, by careful imitation of Euripides, Racine seems to bring French tragedy nearer to what has come to be recognized as the heart of tragedy. Let me use M. Maulnier's words to support this opinion: 'It is in *Iphigénie* that the Racinian concept of fate takes its true shape, that Racine recovers the possibility of using destiny as a force. . . . With *Iphigénie* and *Phèdre* Racine returns to real tragedy . . . the fatality of the Dionysian myth. Once again, by keeping to tradition Racine achieves a revolution, and revives on the French stage the idea of man's unchanging fate.'

If this be any more than an opinion, if it corresponds at all to any real evolution of Racine's mind and art, then *Iphigénie* might well be considered the most important classical play of the seventies. For in it Racine attempts something which he will repeat in *Phèdre* and in *Athalie*, which is a fusion of lucidity and mystery. Up to this point his plays have, one might say, made passion intelligible, not by explaining it away, but by putting it in a full human context. Now he brings into play forces of which man cannot make sense, the inscrutable, the awe-inspiring, the mysterious. In this fusion M. Albert Camus sees the discovery of the truly tragic element in tragedy. In a lecture given in Athens in 1954 he said this: 'Si tout est mystère, il n'y a pas tragédie. Si tout est raison, non plus. La tragédie naît entre l'ombre et la lumière, et par leur opposition' (*Œuvres*, Pléiade, p. 1705). Schiller seems to have reached much the same point in 1804 with *Die Braut von Messina*.

Phèdre is, I suppose, next to *Tartuffe*, the most discussed classical play. In it, as we have seen in Lytton Strachey's words quoted earlier, Racine achieved a magnificence of expression and a tragic power found in no other classical play. From the start it evoked widely differing reactions. Like a mountain peak it does not look the same to all beholders, and is frequently hid by cloud. The fact that it was the last play Racine wrote for public performance has caused the play to be read almost as an *aveu*, a final testimony to the terrible power of passion.

Many such dilemmas are avoided if we approach *Phèdre* as a play written by the poet for whom *Iphigénie* had been a new departure. Even more than that play, *Phèdre* might fit T. S. Eliot's definition of a poem as 'a raid on the inarticulate', using myths once more to present, at a deep level, the effects of passion and the nature of suffering. When in his Preface the poet said that the figure of Phèdre was 'ce que j'ai peut-être mis de plus raisonnable sur le théâtre', I take him to mean, not, of course, that she was a reasonable character but that in describing her suffering he had reached the limit of lucidity as to what could reasonably be said about the human condition. As in *Iphigénie* the King is in the centre of the dramatic picture. One scholar even goes so far as to suggest that 'the terrible events in *Phèdre* are meant for the disillusionment of the only one of the main characters who survives, Thésée, by revealing to him the tragic truth that the gods persecute those they seem to protect' (Leo Spitzer, *Linguistics and Literary History*, p. 88). There is no need for us to adopt this view, any more than we need think of the play as a Jansenistic reading of human nature.

Such divergent interpretations only serve to enforce upon us the wealth of poetic suggestion offered by Racine's finest dramatic poetry.

In the verse of *Phèdre* French classicism seems to reach its ultimate dramatic achievement, allowing us to contemplate the human condition as being in itself tragic. Phèdre is herself torn asunder by natural passion, which is in conflict with her equally natural sense of right. Since the notion of duty and the power to love are both natural, need we look further for tragedy than in this split in human nature as we know it? Tragedy does not happen to us, we do not at certain times become tragic: we are created so. To speak the language of this play, the gods have made us so. In the structure and language of his play Racine has invented a means of contemplating this appalling spectacle, of doing so without revulsion, and yet with a feeling that the poet is right* about our human condition. His picture seems to me to inspire more than that disillusionment that Spitzer found in it; it evokes something akin to 'cette tristesse majesteuse qui fait tout le plaisir de la tragédie'. As Jean Pommier has shown, all these elements—pleasure, dignity, melancholy—are conveyed by Racine's vision of a woman whose conscience is as active as her passion, and whose final speech welcomes death as release.

* His word for this in his preface is *raisonnable*.

8
Biblical Epilogue

DESPITE a recent volume, we do not know much about the death of tragedy. The pertinent words have been spoken by Albert Camus, lecturing in Athens in 1954, who took the view that tragedy is not a type of drama which may be cultivated at will, but a rare and mysterious visitor to western culture, and that our instruments of literary analysis are as yet unable to explain why, three times in some two thousand years, there should have been a brief kindling of the flame of tragic drama.

It is usual to think of the dynamic forces of French classical literature as exhausted by the 1680s. Certainly few plays written in that decade have shown any survival value. The *Andronic* of Campistron was played thirty times in a year, perhaps because it dealt with the theme of Don Carlos, which was to attract Schiller. The *Regulus* of Pradon was even more successful as a drama of Roman patriotism. But for the most part the Paris playgoer of the 1680s had to rely on the old favourites. Mr Lancaster calculates that within the decade *Andromaque* was the most popular play, with 58 performances, *Phèdre* with 51, *Le Cid* with 46, and *Cinna* with 39 (Lancaster, iv. 192).

In retrospect, the chief dramatic development seems to have been, as so often in art, an accident, due to no theatre or group of actors but to Mme de Maintenon, who persuaded Racine to write for her pupils at Saint Cyr, a few miles from Versailles, two Biblical plays. The result was in almost every respect the contrary of the intention.

The experiment was designed for the edification of young ladies: it was said to have endangered their morals. It was planned as a private school play, and it became a political talking point. Mme de La Fayette (admittedly a prejudiced witness) wrote of it that 'ce qui devait être regardé comme une comédie de couvent devint l'affaire la plus sérieuse de la Cour', and that 'tout le monde crut que cette comédie' (i.e. *Esther*) 'était allégorique' (*apud* Orcibal, *La Genèse d''Esther' et d''Athalie'* (1950), pp. 22–3. This remarkable study puts all previous accounts out of date). For the poet also it was an ironical last appearance on the stage. As Maulnier wryly comments, 'Le plus sensuel et le plus terrible des poètes écrit des tragédies pour des petites filles' (*Racine*, p. 255).

It is one of the many strange things about Mme de Maintenon that her idea of a Biblical 'opera' (the word is that of M. Picard) should loosen the tongue of scandal to the extent of seeing in the abandoned courtesan Vashti the figure of Mme de Montespan, and in the wicked Aman a caricature of Louvois. Racine was far too wary a courtier to intend such parallels, yet they were made. Both *Esther* and *Athalie* turned out to be political plays.

The problem is possibly one of our own making. We read allusions into what for Racine was scriptural. We see intentions in what for him may have been no more than a hymn against oppression. That he was pleading the case of a specific group of the oppressed, of the Jansenists, of the Protestants, or (as M. Orcibal thinks) of the congregation of the Filles de Sainte Enfance of Toulouse suppressed in 1686, these are all possible parallels, but unlikely allegories. In any case they have little to do with the literary merit of Racine's last two plays.

The plot of *Esther* is of little interest now. It consists of neatly woven excerpts from the Old Testament source. The spectacle is introduced by the figure of Piety, who refers to 'ce lieu par la Grâce habitée', and the keynote of the action is austerity. The poet underlines the difference between his piece and secular drama:

> Et vous qui vous plaisez aux folles passions
> Qu'allument dans vos cœurs les vaines fictions . . .
> Fuyez de mes plaisirs la sainte austerité;
> Tout respire ici Dieu, la paix, la vérité. (65, 67)

Racine's verse keeps the dignity, and something of the realism, of the Bible. The story of Esther is not a pretty story, 'atroce histoire, pogrom manqué qui se retourne contre ses inspirateurs'. Yet the sense of atmosphere is such that the sufferings of the people of God are conveyed in gentle cadence:

> Quel carnage de toutes parts
> On égorge à la fois les enfants, les vieillards
> Et la sœur et le frère
> Et la fille et la mère
> Le fils dans les bras de son père.
> Que de corps entassés, que de membres épars
> Privés de sépulture
> Grand Dieu, tes saints sont la pâture
> Des tigres et des leopards. (316–)

The sense of the occasion is perfect, but is there, was there ever, any real poetic force in such lines? Some perhaps in these which were nearer to the reality:

> La mer la plus terrible et la plus orageuse
> Est plus sûre pour nous que cette cour trompeuse. (III. i)

And even a little more in the occasional sober image:

> O Dieu, par quelle route inconnue aux mortels
> Ta sagesse conduit ses desseins éternels. (III. viii)

Mme de Sévigné has left on record her impressions of the complete esthetic satisfaction conferred by a royal performance of *Esther*, a pleasure compounded of elegance, milieu, dress, music, diction, the ideal perhaps of classical drama, received with a respect which no Mondory could impose, nor even a Bossuet. No contemporary document conveys so adequately this pleasure; none removes it as effectively from our grasp. For us *Esther* is neither a great nor (except for the specialist) a very interesting play.

But the Court poet was to be allowed one more chance, on condition that the girls should recite and not act his lines. This fact is for us of enormous advantage, since without *Athalie* the history of French classical drama would be a different story. *Esther* was an entertainment, but *Athalie* was a masterpiece. Once more the poet chooses a bloody passage of scripture, and this time it inspired in him the lost art of *Iphigénie*. Some have thought *Athalie* to be Racine's greatest play. Voltaire spoke of it as the ultimate in tragedy, 'le chef d'œuvre de la belle poésie'. To him it conveyed with great force the cruelty of the Church, the spirit of the papacy: 'Grégoire VII (Hildebrand) et Innocent IV ressemblent à Joad.' (Did he not mean Innocent III, who inspired the Fourth Crusade and harried the Albigensians?) What was it that enabled Racine to produce something so much grander than *Esther*, to compose without any prospect of professional acting a tragedy which has been said to treat the most tragic of all subjects, the timeless and eternal revolt of the creature against the creator?

Certainly the subject was no less topical. Controversy over the great and glorious Revolution of 1688 raged around the Lord's Anointed and the fate predicted in Scripture for usurpers, chief among them being Athaliah, presented in the book of Chronicles as persecuting the people of God, and as caught unprotected in the Temple and done to death by the high priest. No wonder that the exiled King James II and his Queen were among the first audiences of *Athalie*.

Visitors to St John's College in Oxford may see as the central portrait behind the high table in hall a figure rather like a Victorian Christ, which is said to be that of William Buckridge, sometime President of the College, Bishop of Ely, and tutor to William Laud. Author of a refutation of Cardinal Bellarmine in 1614 called *De potestate papae in rebus temporalibus*, probably read by Racine, he had proclaimed Athaliah as tyrant, usurper, idolater, and victim. Pamphlet evoked counter-pamphlet at the time of the Rye House Plot, and the controversy reached its height in 1690. (References in Orcibal, op. cit., pp. 136–41.)

All this means that what we now consider as an exception and an after-thought may in fact have been Racine's most 'actual', contemporary play. Just as Dryden presented Monmouth and Shaftesbury in *Absalom and Achitophel* in 1681, so ten years later we may watch Racine offering to exiled Stuarts a theological indictment of their great and successful enemy William III. As in *Esther*, the problem of interpretation is a seventeenth-century problem, it is the problem of an age which had not yet developed a critical attitude to the Bible, and incidentally one that lights up the achievement of the Enlightenment in persuading us that the Bible must and may be read like any other book.

The theme of the tragedy of *Athalie* has never, perhaps, been more clearly expressed than in the New English Bible:

> As soon as Athaliah mother of Ahaziah saw that her son was dead, she set out to extirpate the royal line of the house of Judah. But Jehosheba daughter of King Joram took Ahaziah's son Joash and stole him away from among the princes who were being murdered. . . . Thus Jehosheba . . . hid Joash from Athaliah so that she did not put him to death. . . .
>
> Then they brought out the king's son . . . and Jehoida and his sons anointed him. . . . When Athaliah heard the noise of the people . . . she came into the house of the Lord where the people were and found the king standing on the dais. . . . Athaliah rent her clothes and cried, 'Treason! Treason!' Jehoida the priest gave orders to the captains in command of the troops: 'Bring her outside the precincts and let anyone in attendance on her be put to the sword'. . . . So they laid hands on her and took her to the royal palace and killed her there at the passage to the Horse Gate.
>
> (2 Chronicles, 22:10, 23:11)

Such is the narrow basis on which Racine constructs his tragedy, very much as he had constructed *Bérénice* in 1670. The issues are conveyed by the *confidents*, by Mathan, a renegade Israelite, by Abner, Athaliah's general, and above all by Joad the high priest and by the Queen herself. Once again we watch the tragic split between principles and protagonists, each side being treated with fairness and allowed the full statement of its case. The pitiless protagonists are surrounded by a chorus of Levite girls who interpret the action, confident in the power of God, which for Racine and his age was the most obvious and impressive thing in the Bible.

The tragic struggle depends on the fact that Athalie faces enemies both without and within. Joad, her chief antagonist, is no more powerful than the voice of conscience that lames her will. There is no peace for the wicked, says the Bible, and the poet turns the fact into drama:

> Fuyez tout ce tumulte et dans votre palais
> A vos sens agités venez rendre la paix.

Non, je ne puis; tu vois mon trouble et ma faiblesse.
Va, fais dire à Mathan qu'il vienne, qu'il se presse.
Heureuse si je puis trouver par son secours
Cette paix que je cherche et qui me fuit toujours. (II. iii)

This distracted mortal regards God less as her Maker than as her
adversary, an unfair foe, since he holds all the cards:

Impitoyable Dieu, toi seul as tout conduit.
C'est toi qui me flattant d'une vengeance aisée
M'a vingt fois en un jour à moi-même opposée
Tantôt pour un enfant excitant mes remords,
Tantôt m'éblouissant le tes riches tresors,
Que j'ai craint de livrer aux flammes, au pillage.
Qu'il règne donc ce fils, ton soin et ton ouvrage,
Et que pour signaler son empire nouveau
On lui fasse en mon sein enfoncer le couteau.
Voici ce qu'en mourant lui souhaite sa mère.
Que dis-je souhaiter, je me flatte, j'espère
Qu'indocile à ton joug, fatigué de ta loi,
Fidèle au sang d'Achab qu'il a reçu de moi,
Conforme à son aïeul, à son pere semblable,
On verra de David l'héritier détestable
Abolir tes honneurs, profaner tes autels,
Et venger Athalie, Achab et Jezabel. (V. vi)

These magnificent lines give me much more than a version of a
supposedly edifying portion of Scripture. With true dramatic
instinct they allow to the character about to die a final curse, such
as Corneille had given to Camille and Racine to Agrippina. The
downfall of the wicked is much more impressive when the wicked
have a case and are allowed to state it. To believe in the final defeat
of God was for Racine no doubt an impiety almost too painful to
contemplate, but to find in the Biblical text such an attitude stimulated the poet in him to express, and in what grand terms, a defiance
which was both doomed and desperate. Athalie in his hand is thus
a counterpart of Milton's Satan, on the wrong side maybe, but a
living adversary, the more dramatic in that she is unafraid. (Molière
had suggested certain features of such an attitude in the figure of

Don Juan.) For anything comparable to the eloquence of Athalie
we must go to *Paradise Lost*:

> What though the field be lost?
> All is not lost; the unconquerable will
> And study of revenge, immortal hate
> And courage never to submit or yield.

Have not Milton and Racine in mind the same kind of conflict?
And is it not, in dramatic terms, the most tragic conflict that may
be imagined? It is the tragic outcome of free will, that human
attribute which had inspired so much controversy, but which in
poetry was not argued so much as it was shown, in its impressive
strength, in its irony, in its self-contradictory and thus illusory
violence, the eternal conflict of the creature against the creator. A
modern actor finds in Racine's play just this, 'la tragédie éternelle
des rapports du Créateur et de l'homme, le moment qui ne cesse
point'.

Incidentally, is not this the final word about the unity of time?
Does it not explain why pedants, and dramatists in their wake, had
argued so tediously about how long a play should take? There is of
course no single answer, since some spectators are conscious of time
passing and some are not. But the answer of the poet Racine is
hardly in doubt. The tragic moment envisaged in *Phèdre* and
Athalie is one of essence, not sequence; the conflict is not something
that occurs and that may therefore cease; it is a conflict in the nature
of man. Even to call it eternal is not appropriate, since the very
idea of duration is absent. For Racine the nature of man, human
nature, is in its essence and structure tragic. With greater justice,
perhaps, than a modern Spaniard he could have called his whole
work 'The Tragic Sense of Life', and in a private play commis-
sioned as edification he seems to have found a subject able to furnish
him with his deepest accents and most subtle insights. This tragic
sense of life has not been possible since the seventeenth century,
and we should be grateful that Racine and his public were un-
touched by the rationalism that turned the Bible into a book like
any other. For the Enlightenment such a poetic figure as the Aveng-
ing Angel, 'L'ange exterminateur', which seemed to brood over

E

the last Act of Racine's play, would have been unintelligible, as it may well be to us.

There is some evidence that one or two of Racine's contemporaries had a sense of what was happening. The aged Boileau, in whom Addison in 1701 found a wonderful vigour, wrote in the twelfth of his *Reflexions Critiques sur Longin*, after quoting four lines (61–4) from *Athalie*, that French had recaptured that magnificence of style which the ancients called sublime: 'En effet, tout ce qu'il peut y avoir de sublime paraît rassemblé dans ces quatre vers: la grandeur de la pensée, la noblesse du sentiment, la magnificence des paroles et l'harmonie de l'expression.'

9
The Form Described

IT is time to consider the means whereby all the plays we have been discussing were conveyed to their audience, and are now conveyed to their readers. With rare exceptions, such as *L'Avare*, that means is verse, rhyming verse, verse of a kind which it is not easy for English readers to appreciate, which goes by the name of the Alexandrine. Rhyme, as Chapelain said, is an enemy of realism, and (one would think) of drama also. No statement can sound either natural or independent if it is obviously expressed in such a way as to rhyme with the following statement. Even that great play *Tartuffe* has a most lame beginning:

> Allons, Flipote, allons, que d'eux je me délivre
> — Vous marchez d'un tel pas qu'on a peine à vous suivre.

I recollect an unfortunate attempt to convey to a class a Racinian motif by reading the English verse translation by Nathaniel Lee: the rhymes produced laughter and any tragic atmosphere was impossible. On the other hand, I must bear testimony that one is rarely aware of this handicap; the skill of the French dramatists in handling their rhymes is second only to the ease with which they seem to have written, at speed, thousands of lines. Even the prose of *L'Avare* is at times in verse groupings.

What is really unfortunate is the prejudice felt by many beginners towards the actual measure of French verse. The French Alexandrine is still often spoken of as a monotonous measure. English critics who should have known better have been rude about it, and

certainly the tradition of recitation at the *Comédie Française* used
to be sing-song and declamatory, much more so probably in the
seventeenth century. But the Alexandrine has two major advantages
as a form of dramatic speech. It is a measure without any scheme of
scansion such as bars or feet, and its stress varies with meaning.
Many people rob themselves of much pleasure by not knowing that
the Alexandrine is more free than the iambic pentameter. It consists
of lines of twelve syllables arranged in alternating couplets, the
feminine one having in effect thirteen syllables because of the
feminine ending. The great majority of lines have a pause in the
middle, so that a full line might be called two lines of six syllables.
Now six is the normal number of syllables in a breath-group. That
experienced teacher Henri Berthon would make his students analyse
passages from Bossuet, and the natural groups were five, seven,
occasionally four or eight, but normally around six. To pronounce
syllables as groups of six ('hemistich' is the usual name for this)
would indeed be monotonous, but this never happens. A normal
Alexandrine comes to the ear in four parts, with a major pause after
the six, and minor but most significant pauses within each six. This,
of course, does not make it poetic, but dramatic speech need not
always be poetic. Prosaic things have to be said, and the Alexandrine
allows them to be said, nearly as easily as prose would do. For
instance,

> Chacun sait aujourd'hui quand il fait de la prose.

This is an Alexandrine of a perfectly regular type, with a break half-
way along, and minor breaks, if desired, at *sait* and *fait*. Exactly the
same, in fact, as this:

> Un destin plus heureux vous conduit en Epire,

but not quite the same as this:

> Il ouvre un large bec, laisse tomber sa proie

—in which the natural pauses would probably fall after the second,
sixth, and seventh syllables (i.e. 2, 4; 1, 5).

Some of the more subtle effects of French classical verse are
attained by the slight shift in the minor pauses. A repetition, for

instance, will be stressed on the second syllable of the first hemistich, but on the third of the second, thus:

> Je meurs si je vous perds mais je meurs si j'attends,

or this:

> Que le jour recommence et que le jour finisse.

Both Racine and Corneille exploit at times the dramatic value of a
stressed first syllable:

> Rome n'est plus dans Rome, elle est toute où je suis.
> — Ah, ne puis-je savoir si j'aime ou si je hais.

Or of stress upon the first syllable of the second hemistich:

> Un désordre éternel | règne dans son esprit.

To keep even the 6 : 6 division would ruin such a line as this:

> Je ne t'ai point aimé, cruel qu'ai-je donc fait?

and perhaps this also:

> Oui, Monsieur a raison, Madame, il faut choisir
> (*Misanthrope*, 1603. The editions put a colon after *raison*)

This then is the instrument. For us it is the gateway into classical
drama. We cannot enter save by this door. If we fail to appreciate
its potential, if we are put off by the artifice, if we find the diction
at times too near prose, we are denying ourselves much pleasure,
for in perfecting the Alexandrine the French have, I think,
responded to a sure dramatic instinct. They have cultivated a
regular form of measured speech, removed from the speech of the
everyday world, but which allows all the dramatic effects of speech:
it can be direct, prosaic, laconic, even inconsequent. Molière gives
us within the classical measure the helplessness of incoherence that
cannot even be grammatical:

> C'est un homme . . . qui . . . ha . . . un homme . . . un homme enfin

or

> Nous verrons si c'est moi que vous voudrez qui sorte.

The great point is that it is speech adapted to what it had to do, to the nature of classical drama. The physical action of Elizabethan drama would have been too much for it, but 'la conception essentiellement classique de l'art . . . veut que le drame soit un jeu de sentiments ayant une portée universelle' (Vinaver, *Racine*, p. 13). If the drama had to show us Horatius defending Rome or killing his sister, then rhetorical verse would be no fit medium. For mental reaction to such events, rhetoric is no bad medium:

> C'est trop, ma patience à la raison fait place,
> Va dedans les enfers plaindre ton Curiace.

It is no accident that the dramatic subjects suit the verse, as conversely the verse brings out the emotive shock of the subjects. To say, for example, that

> Rodrigue dans mon cœur combat encor mon père

is not to invent a pretty conceit, but to put rhetoric to its proper use, that of describing mental conflict, which, even in Corneille's play, is nearer the subject of the conflict than any duel.

Anything that has a local habitation and a name seems inimical to classical drama. Its best subjects all avoid physical encounter, they avoid events and individuals; they treat 'the heart of the matter', the clash of views, ambitions, moods. We soon find out that the one can be as dramatic as the other. All we need to do is to avoid asking 'English' questions, such as 'who is this?' or 'where are we?' The French poet answers the first by removing Phèdre as far as possible from history and geography into legend, and by describing her as 'la fille de Minos et de Pasiphaé'. He answers the second by substituting for it the more emotional question: 'who is here?' It does not matter where we are. Dramatically what matters is whether we are near the one person whom I long, or dread, to see.

> Allons, qu'il vienne enfin.
> — Madame, le voici.
> Ah, je ne croyais pas qu'il fût si près d'ici.
>   (*Andromaque*, 475)

Even more in the manner of a *coup de théâtre*:

Il ne me verra plus.
— Madame, le voici.

In her admirable analysis of this aspect of Racinian drama, Mme de
Mourgues says: 'The place chosen has no real existence, in the
ordinary meaning of the word, but only an ideal, symbolic existence,
like the drawing-room which stands for hell in Sartre's *Huis Clos*.
Its only *raison d'être* seems to be that human beings should be
thrown together, to torture one another without any possible escape'
(*Racine*, p. 24).

It is common to speak of classical drama as 'ruled' by the unity of
time. But this, in the hands of the chief French artists, is not imposed: it is an aspect of the dramatic concentration upon essential
intellectual and emotional elements which a normal time sequence
would only disturb. In Racine the 'rule' is seen to be a deep esthetic
requirement. It never occurred to d'Aubignac that time is frighten-
ing, that one may live in the past (like Agrippina) or in the future
(like Agamemnon). What will happen is juxtaposed ironically to
what is:

Ils ne se verront plus.
—Ils s'aimeront toujours.

For this kind of dramatic poetry the verse is an admirably contrived medium. It can mirror the intellectual elements of a situation;
it can, by the device of the hemistich, enforce comparison, contrast,
separation, opposition. 'The verse itself realises in every detail the
action of the whole . . . In the perfect balance of the rhymed couplet,
in the perfect balance of the individual line (regularly though not
invariably broken in the middle) one feels the logical form of
thesis and antithesis, the tragic split between reason and passion'
(Fergusson, *Idea of a Theater*, p. 66).

One might think that such a form would be a vehicle more suited
to tragedy than to comedy, which seems to be anchored to the particular, the individual, the precise detail. Yet a great comic poet has
used the Alexandrine apparently without strain, and one of the
delights of studying Molière is to see how the apparently local is
made into classical poetry. To say that these plays generalize situations is unfortunate, since when anything is generalized it loses

point and savour. But fools in Molière keep their physical attributes. Tartuffe is a glutton even though we do not see him eating. His sexual appetite is declared even in his assumed asceticism:

> Couvrez ce sein que je ne saurais voir.

Harpagon is a distracted man, and betrays his anguish as he looks . . . at the audience:

> Quel bruit fait-on là-haut? Est-ce mon voleur qui y est? De grâce, si l'on sait des nouvelles de mon voleur, je supplie qu'on m'en dise.

Jean Vilar confessed after years of stage experience that he had reached the view that the only way to play *L'Avare* was as a farce.

So, even in the classical mode, comedy keeps something of its physical setting. But only something. These physical attributes are subordinate to a dramatic clash as sharp as any in Corneille and Racine. They serve, in fact, an intellectual end. The point about Tartuffe's lubricity is that it is absurd. It is greater than he thinks, greater even than his skill of deception. To have one's pastiche of holiness spoilt by one's all-too-human appetite is a classical comic subject.

Adventures into the absurd, such might be a covering title for classical comedy. Why then the restricting form? For Molière it was no restriction, because it was optional. His plays vary in length, they use prose as well as verse, they admit music and dance; they even break, as we have just seen from *L'Avare*, the dramatic illusion. The delightful opening of *Les Fâcheux* is a case of this:

> Just before the curtain rose one of the actors (you might say myself) appeared on stage in ordinary dress and, addressing the King with the look on his face of a man caught unawares, made a few untidy excuses for being on his own, without time to have rehearsed his colleagues for the entertainment which the King seemed to expect. As he spoke, from a score of fountains there opened out the shell that everyone knows about, and the pretty maiden within it came to the edge of the stage and declaimed in the grand style the lines written by M. Pellisson as Prologue.

Such a freedom of form avoids the stilted grandeur of the tragic mode. It allows comedy to be informal, human, natural, yet never disordered or unplanned. It allows free play to the fantasy which will imagine the outward form of a doctor, the gown, the pointed hat, while the man beneath is a wood-cutter, without medical knowledge, without any academic means of avoiding the traps and pitfalls, with only his wits to rescue him. Such a fantasy offers for our pleasure speech, academic speech, without content, the jargon is about . . . nothing:

> Hippocrate dit . . . que nous nous couvrions tous deux.
> — Hippocrate dit cela?
> — Oui.
> — Dans quel chapitre, s'il vous plaît?
> — Dans son chapitre . . . des chapeaux.
> — Puisque Hippocrate le dit, il le faut faire.
>
> (Le Médécin malgré lui, II. iii)

Just as in the heroic language of tragedy no statement is too fantastic, so the absurdities of comedy are allowed to run into a riot of language, which has no footing in reality, but to which a rogue can impart a tone of conviction. Thus Scapin:

Va, va, nous partagerons les périls en frères; et trois ans de galères de plus ou de moins ne sont pas pour arrêter un noble cœur. (I. 7)

Non, non, ne me pardonnez rien; passez-moi votre épée à travers le corps. Je serai ravi que vous me tuiez. (II. 7)

Et moi, qu'on me porte au bout de la table, en attendant que je meure.
(III. 14)

Let us watch this fantasy at work on a larger canvas, in the language put in the mouth of a character who, like Tartuffe, has chosen hypocrisy as a way of life. He gives a new twist to the legend of Don Juan:

Beneath this useful cover I shall disappear and make sure of my schemes. I shall not give up my pleasant way of life, but shall take care to remain unnoticed and have my pleasure unobtrusively. If I am found out, I shall find without difficulty that a strong party will take charge of my interests and be my defence against one and all. In a word, this is the way to do as I like without interference. (V. 2)

If we watch the structure of Molière's *Dom Juan*, we begin to see a comic subject developed with that care for 'le nécessaire' which Corneille thought essential for tragedy. As the series of encounters unfolds before us, we see that all are necessary: each one suggests a freedom of the aristocrat which is a scandal to any social sense. Each one is a form of doing what he confessed to his servant he aimed to do: 'faire impunément tout ce que je voudrai'. So he cuts himself free, from promises of marriage, from obeying the scriptural injunction 'swear not at all', from paying a tradesman, from respect of parents, from believing in anything but the present. Could the *idea* of libertinage be more firmly presented? Is this freedom really that of an *esprit fort*? Or was La Bruyère right that 'l'esprit fort c'est l'esprit faible'? There is little doubt in our minds, as we watch Molière's presentation, that he gives an ironical view of this so-called freedom. His play gives dramatic form, one might say, to the paradox which Pascal has compressed into a single line: 'rien n'est si lâche que de faire le brave contre Dieu.' As Guicharnaud says: 'Le personnage est de plain-pied avec lui-même, et clos . . . libéré de tout, sauf de son appétit, dont il est en revanche totalement prisonnier' (*Molière*, pp. 198–9).

It is an old prejudice that comedy must be centred on a comic character, as tragedy centres on 'a' protagonist. Classical comedy is not so restricted. The heart of the comedy in *Dom Juan* is less in the sketch of a *libertin* (let alone a libertine) than in an opposition, between the free man and the serving man. Sganarelle is the Sancho Panza of French literature. His master's incredulity he counters by being credulous and cowardly and superstitious. As the Don mocks at religion so Sganarelle goes in fear of dark powers, bogey-men, and spirits. Let us not forget that this contrast was offered to a society officially religious, where one was not free to profess unbelief. Only on the stage was any freedom of utterance possible, and the play was removed after the fifteenth performance.

Who is the comic figure in *Tartuffe*? Nobody has been able to answer this question, because the play rests on two comic figures. In the first draft of three Acts this was probably not so. The farce was played around the folly of Orgon, whose common sense deserted him as soon as religion was concerned, to the point of allowing the crook to see as much as he liked of Orgon's wife. But the finished play is a far more subtle structure. Orgon is still a fool, ready to accept inhumanity in the name of religion

> Il m'enseigne à n'avoir affection pour rien . . .
> Et je verrais mourir frère, enfants, mère et femme . . . (276, 278)

rather than to use his eyes to discover what is going on under his nose. But the impostor clever enough to dupe him is himself a dupe, the slave of gross carnal appetite. To leave us in no doubt about this we are given two love scenes, two glimpses of the impostor in private, where he can say what he feels and not what he pretends. The man whom Orgon took to be a saint because of his admissions of sin has in fact no sense of sin:

> Le scandale du monde est ce qui fait l'offence
> Et ce n'est pas pécher que pécher en silence. (1505-6)

This is so far from the usual tone of comedy that it has been interpreted as satire. But the economy of the play leaves no doubt that Molière was using the classical form to develop a confrontation rather than to attack an enemy. Orgon's brother, in a long and careful speech, had taxed him with mixing up black and white—

> rendre même honneur au masque qu'au visage
> Égaler l'artifice à la sincérité
> Confondre l'apparence avec la vérité. (334-6)

The language, the verse, the care to distinguish concepts, are all part of the classical form. The real subject is the mask of piety and its relation to the face of truth. The first version showed, thanks to the folly of the recipient, the mask as powerful as the truth. The final version shows the mask as inadequate for the wearer. As Arnolphe's scheme collapsed because of his own humanity, so Tartuffe's assumption of holiness cannot be maintained when his sensuality is awakened. It is illuminating to see how sensuality is presented in this play. Not so much evil as natural, genuine; it is the one thing about Tartuffe that is not assumed, put on, manufactured. The play allows us to argue that the impostor's own nature prevents his evil scheme from succeeding. This would be to import into the play a moral which Molière was not, as far as we know, anxious to stress.

The theory of all this finds its most satisfying expression, not in Molière but in Pascal. *Tartuffe* seems to me to illustrate Pascal's epigram on the war between our brain and our body, our intelligence and our nature:

Je mets en fait qu'il n'y a jamais eu de pyrrhonien effectif parfait. La nature soutient la raison impuissante et l'empêche d'extravaguer jusqu'à ce point.

(Pascal, ed. minor, p. 530)

The mind may mislead us but the body can prevent our being misled beyond a certain point. Does not *Tartuffe* bear out this view? In the course of the *Lettre sur 'L'Imposteur'*, which I take to incorporate Molière's theory of his play, and of the kind of classical comedy of which it was but one example, the new principle is expressed thus: 'incongruity is the essence of the comic, and . . . it follows that all forms of lying, disguise, trickery, dissimulation, appearance belying fact, incompatible acts deriving from a single source, these are in essence comic' (GE, iv. 569).

We have not, perhaps, paid sufficient attention to the last two words of this quotation. They tell us what in Molière's view was the essence of the comic. In this case it is the substitution of the appearance for the fact, the unreal passing for the real. If we take Molière seriously here we shall watch for the same plan in his other plays. We shall see how he uses the classical form in *Dom Juan* to show a man living in a world of his own, a world without morality, a world of his brain, a world which his nature might have shown him to be an illusion.

Does not Molière's greatest experiment with classical form show this at a deep level? *Le Misanthrope* is a play built on contrasts. A man protests against social hypocrisy. His protest is total, doctrinaire, excessive in that it takes no account of his own fallibility. He presents to the world a case, a theory, with considerable basis in fact, but which is vitiated by the assumption that he is right and all the others wrong, all the time. This is absurd. Absurd to the point of making him regret being in love, making him resist his natural politeness, making him as doctrinaire in literary matters as he is in morals. The play presents the doctrinaire as comic, because and in so far as it is unnatural, contrary to nature. By nature Alceste is polite:

> J'ai le défaut
> D'être un peu plus sincère en cela qu'il ne faut. (300)

This is a calm statement, but when angry his tone is different. If others find good things to say about *précieux* poems, 'C'est qu'ils ont l'art de feindre; et moi, je ne l'ai pas.' In the grip of his theory he indicts the entire human race. This is classical comedy. It is not an individual being funny; it is not the study of a type such as we have seen for instance in *Les Visionnaires*. It is, if you will, a study of a nonconformist; it shows the anti-social effects of sustaining a principle, a good principle, but doing so extravagantly, without compromise, or patience, or a sense of honour, or humility. A man who acts thus is rated by the rest of society as an 'extravagant', as a man without judgement, without that quality which Montaigne thought most valuable of all human attributes. The victim glories in being condemned by a world which he has come to despise, and which in the end he has to leave. Just so did Arnolphe, and George Dandin, who is forced to the conclusion that the only reasonable course open to him is suicide: 'Quand le héros molièresque s'est enfin aperçu que le monde résiste inexorablement à son vœu, il ne peut que disparaître' (Guicharnaud, op. cit., p. 494). This is not an incursion of tragedy, as some have thought. It is the logical end of folly that flies in the face of facts and nature and social reality. The protest that seemed so clever and so right ends in a solitude which need not be, but which is the height of the grotesque.

Such is the content of what some take to be the greatest French play. That content is so closely wedded to a verse form both lucid and suggestive that it is hard to see any dividing line. These puppets —for they are no more—ape human attitudes, in words that judge those attitudes. Each in his own way bears witness to what one of them called 'Ce grand aveuglement où chacun est pour soi' (968). The verse, the monologues, the unexpected escape of the truth, these all show the classical form in its perfection, suggesting the mystery behind decision and the paradoxical fragility of reason. 'L'homme croit se conduire lorsqu'il est conduit.' Alceste, the idealist, the rigorist, was brought to see this was so:

> Je ne suis plus à moi, je suis tout à la rage, ...
> Mes sens par la raison ne sont plus gouvernés. (1310, 1312)

M. Guicharnaud's studies culminate in the suggestion that the greater comedies show what he calls 'Molière ou les dangers de la nature' (p. 527). Perhaps we have been unjust to their immediate influence. For they were watched, no doubt, by one who, as we have seen, was to compose strikingly similar pictures of the limits of the human condition, but in the tragic mode.

What did Racine learn from Molière? We shall never know, but the scene in *Mithridate* where the father lays a trap for the son, as did Harpagon, may be a direct tribute. Voltaire thought so, and Gustave Rudler seems to agree: 'la proximité des dates (1668, 1673) et l'inoubliable éclat des scènes de Molière lui donnent de la vraisemblance' (Racine, *Mithridate*, ed. Rudler, p. xxvi). It may be no accident that Racine's impressive pictures of the tragic possibilities in our human condition were imagined in Paris during the years in which Molière was imagining in the comic mode something similar. If we ask what it is that leads the tragic character to disaster, we get much the same answer in both cases. The character pursues an end which is either unattainable or disastrous. Hermione and Roxane not only pursue their own unhappiness: they decide to do what they do not wish to do:

> Je tremble au seul penser du coup qui le menace (1405),

and again:

> ... ne voyais-tu pas, dans mes comportements,
> Que mon cœur démentait ma bouche à tous moments?
> (*Andromaque*, 1547–8)

But, at a deeper level, Phèdre. Only the Alexandrine measure, perhaps, could use the rhetoric to present the thought at one remove, so to say, from the speaker:

> Que fais-je? Où ma raison se va t-elle égarer? (1264)

This is a picture of a human being appalled at the crimes to which her lover is driving her, as she was appalled at the way she had come to hate the most natural part of her, her affection. For it was love that drove her to crime:

> Ce n'est plus une ardeur dans mes veines cachée
> C'est Venus tout entière à sa proie attachée
> J'ai conçu pour mon crime une juste terreur
> J'ai pris la vie en haine, et ma flamme en horreur. (305–9)

When a scholar takes these lines seriously, can we wonder that he interprets them as an indictment of the order of the world? It is the gods who make us love, and who give us at the same time conscience and a sense of right. Yet if the conflict of love and duty be raised to its maximum the human person will be consumed. Jean-Louis Barrault produces the play so that at the end Phèdre shall be just that, *entièrement consumée*.

This is not the place to explain the mysteries of modern tragedy. We can here only remark that a verse form which in fact both expresses and contains violence is the perfect vehicle for a tragic subject. Indeed, it may be said to make the subject. Racine's tragedy is not the recital of the events which befell a mythical queen: it is the critical expression of dynamic qualities in conflict. Critical, because the verse has to show, and only such verse can show, 'les dangers de la nature'.

There are many subjects that classical drama cannot attempt. Disorder that is not counterbalanced or contained is beyond the power of verse to present. Issues that involve length of time and multiplicity of participants are beyond its range. But simplify the issue, present it on a basis of the unified personality, and these classical creations are possible. One may say that classical drama pleases by the clarity it confers on possibilities of the grotesque and the disastrous. This clarity has not been possible in Europe since the seventeenth century. The visions of a Dostoievski need another, and a more epic, medium.

But what, in the last analysis, do we mean by such epithets as 'grotesque' and 'disastrous'? They describe two forms of the impossible. Here we touch the nerve of classical French drama. Its themes all seem to point to dramatic confrontations with the impossible. Such confrontation is bound to be dramatic in the highest degree. Since mortals can only accomplish the possible, any challenge by the impossible must reduce them to absurdity, or to ruin. These are two forms of defeat: to be absurd is to be intellectually defeated; to die in failure is to be mortally defeated. The comic and the tragic modes envisage the same thing: they are, as it were, two angles of vision of the human predicament.

Not only so, but the cause of the absurdity and of the disaster is the same confidence in human power to satisfy the ego. 'L'amour-propre rend les hommes idolâtres d'eux mêmes . . . on ne peut sonder la profondeur ni percer les ténèbres de ses abîmes.' Is not the comedy of *George Dandin* an attempt to plumb these depths?

> This is my great moment, and now I can put down your pride and expose your tricks. Up to now you have made light of my complaints, thrown dust in the eyes of your parents, and covered your dishonesty. No matter what I saw, no matter what I said, your skill always found a way round my rights; you were always clever enough to win. But this time we shall see how matters really stand, and your impudence will be shown up for what it is. (GE, vi. 579)

We laugh at the words of a silly man, who seems responsible for his own predicament. But is he? Is not his position a (comic) suggestion of our own? Not only silly men are exasperated by the gap between their due and its realization in practice. The desire to have things straight, and to be shown right when one is right . . . this is no laughing matter, it is comedy, of a deep kind. It is a suggestion of the Baudelairean gap between dream and act.

Is not *Britannicus* another such attempt, showing us, in Nero and Agrippina, people impelled by their biological *amour-propre*, the one to demand, the other to resist? Pale characters like Narcissus and Britannicus do not direct the action; they are the means, the occasion allowing the personality to go to the full extent of self-assertion; but this means, to their ruin.

The French tragic vision lights up terrifying possibilities in our human condition. Its vision of what man is has a more powerful effect upon us than anything that man does. Chance in this drama reveals us to ourselves. 'Nescimus saepe quod possumus set tentatio aperit quid sumus.' Corneille read this in the *Imitatio Christi*—probably after he had put many instances of it into his plays. La Rochefoucauld may have noticed it in both the treatise and the plays: 'La fortune fait paraître nos vertus et nos vices comme la lumière fait paraître les objets' (*Maxime*, 380). Does not such a tragic figure as Roxane strike us as created by a poet who had meditated the fatal consequences of chance? She is seen as for a moment free, by the absence of her master, as Phèdre is for a moment freed by the report of the king's death. But both are free to show what they really are. Their so-called freedom reveals the truth that otherwise they would have done anything to conceal.

A Note on Further Reading

It was once the fashion in universities to give reading lists. I prefer to let a student go through the process many of us have had to undergo in preparing our doctoral thesis: that is to discover source books for ourselves, and to watch the chronological advance of research as we come to realize what our subject involves. Others think that valuable time is saved if some leading books are commended at the start.

An excellent corrective to the notion that literary study must confine itself to books, in this case 'French' books of a bygone age, is supplied by Anthony Blunt in his volume of the Pelican History of Art dealing with the sixteenth and seventeenth centuries, *French Art and Architecture* (2nd edn., 1957). Stimulating also are the two works of Aldous Huxley dealing with France in the seventeenth century, *Grey Eminence* and *The Devils of Loudun* (1941 and 1952).

Documentation prior to the Second World War is put out of date by Professor Antoine Adam's imposing volumes, *Histoire de la littérature française au 17e siecle* (1947–53). Invaluable as a record of extant plays is H. Carrington Lancaster's *History of French Dramatic Literature in the Seventeenth Century* (10 vols., 1929–42). Work on the Paris theatres is reported in the *Revue de l'histoire du théâtre*, and treated in particular in the works of Mme Deierkauf-Holsboer: *Histoire de la mise-en-scène, Histoire du théâtre du Marais, Histoire de l'Hôtel de Bourgogne*, etc. No good or complete history of the Comédie Française is known to me, but this theatre as we know it dates from an amalgamation of 1680; as such, it would hardly come into this book. Documents of a legal nature have been collected by Mme Jurgens and Miss Maxfield-Miller in *Cent Ans de recherches sur Molière* (1963), and by M. Picard in his *Corpus Racinianum* (1956). Invaluable for press notices etc. are the two volumes of P. Mélèse on *Le Théâtre et le public, 1659–1715* (1934). The plays themselves can in many cases be read in pleasant modern editions: for instance, in the Classiques Garnier, Textes Français Modernes, Éditions du Seuil, Clarendon French Series, the Textes Français of the University of London Press, and those of the house of Harrap.

The main artists have been abundantly treated, but recent works seem to have been more critical than scholarly in tendency, by which I mean that a view of the author has been imposed on analysis of his work. This would apply in my view to the books of Doubrowsky on Corneille, of Arnavon on Molière, and of Goldmann and Jasinski on Racine. I have found more enlightenment in the work of Vedel, *Deux Classiques français* (1935); Picard, *La Carrière de Racine* (1956); Guicharnaud, *Molière* (1963); R. C. Knight, *Racine et la Grèce* (1950); P. France, *Racine's Rhetoric* (1965); and Odette de Mourgues, *Racine, or the Triumph of Relevance* (1967). My own enjoyment of Racine is chiefly due to the small volume of Thierry Maulnier, and to the work of Lytton Strachey in *Books and Characters* (1922) and *Landmarks in French Literature* (1912; OPUS edn., 1969).

More general works that will prove helpful are Peacock, *The Art of Drama* (1957); J. Morel, *La Tragédie* (1969); L. J. Potts, *(Comedy* (1949); T. Niklaus, *Harlequin Phoenix* (1956), and the essay by George Meredith on *The Idea of Comedy and the Uses of the Comic Spirit* (1897).

Index